BASKETBALL NOW!

BASKETBALL NOW!

THE STARS AND STORIES OF THE NBA

ADAM ELLIOTT SEGAL

THIRD EDITION

FIREFLY BOOKS

A Firefly Book

Published by Firefly Books Ltd. 2019
Copyright © 2019 Firefly Books Ltd.
Text copyright © 2019 Adam Elliott Segal
Photographs © as listed on page 159

First printing

Library of Congress Control Number: 2019940488

Library and Archives Canada Cataloguing in Publication
Title: Basketball now! : the stars and stories of the NBA /
    Adam Elliott Segal.
Names: Segal, Adam Elliott, author.
Description: Third edition.
Identifiers: Canadiana 20190129387 | ISBN 9780228102021 (softcover)
Subjects: LCSH: National Basketball Association. |
    LCSH: Basketball players—United States—Biography. |
    LCSH: Basketball players—United States. |
    LCSH: Basketball—United States—History.
Classification: LCC GV884.A1 S44 2019 | DDC 796.323092/273—dc23

Published in the United States by
Firefly Books (U.S.) Inc.
P.O. Box 1338, Ellicott Station
Buffalo, New York 14205

Published in Canada by
Firefly Books Ltd.
50 Staples Avenue, Unit 1
Richmond Hill, Ontario L4B 0A7

Cover design: Noor Majeed
Interior design: Matt Filion (third edition updates by Stacey Cho)

Printed in Canada

Canadä

We acknowledge the financial support of the Government of Canada.

CONTENTS

INTRODUCTION

IN THE MIDDLE of North America's worst polar vortex in a generation, things in the NBA started heating up. It was Super Bowl week 2019, but for once, hardly anyone on talk radio or television was talking about Tom Brady and the New England Patriots. No, this week the NBA was the focus, and the craziest week of the season began with the Unibrow and ended with a unicorn.

Anthony Davis, the New Orleans Pelicans' franchise player, announced that he wanted out. Management was rightfully concerned — Davis was still under contract — and fireworks ensued when it surfaced that the Lakers, the new home of LeBron James, was Davis' preferred destination. This really started in the 2018 off-season, when James bolted from Cleveland to Hollywood after another finals loss to the Golden State Warriors. Like his move to Miami in 2010, James' change of address started a chain reaction across the league, with superstars and role players alike trying to follow the King wherever he landed. Everyone, including Davis, wants to win titles alongside LeBron.

That same week in January, another bombshell dropped. A blockbuster deal saw the New York Knicks send Kristaps Porzingis, aka the Unicorn, to the Dallas Mavericks for Dennis Smith Jr. and a cast of expiring contracts. The deal cleared enough cap space for New York to land future primo free agents and potentially reboot the franchise. As the All-Star break loomed, this one week spotlighted both the top teams and struggling franchises in the league. And that's the thing with the NBA — there is always something going on!

Soon came the NBA trade deadline, one of the craziest on record. The Toronto Raptors and Milwaukee Bucks both made mega moves, with Toronto picking up All-Star center Marc Gasol and Milwaukee nabbing sharpshooter Nikola Mirotic. The east, for the first time in recent memory, was LeBron-less, and middle-market teams were seeking to capitalize on a chance for a championship run.

Aside from the off-court circus, there was also some actual basketball being played on actual basketball courts! Make no mistake, the Raptors were the talk of the league since the first tipoff in 2018–19. Toronto surged quickly to first overall in the east with the addition of Kawhi Leonard, who joined the team after a blockbuster move in the 2018 off-season that had Toronto trading longtime Raptor DeMar DeRozan to San Antonio. Although Kyrie Irving righted the tilting Celtics ship midway through the season and the Milwaukee Bucks eventually supplanted Toronto as the best team in the Eastern Conference under the MVP-winning efforts of the Greek Freak, Giannis Antetokounmpo, the Raptors would have the last laugh. The surging Philadelphia 76ers, with the deadly combo of Joel Embiid and Ben Simmons, might have toppled Toronto in the second round of the playoffs if not for Leonard's off-the-rim series-winning buzzer beater. Look, this is a "make or miss" league, as the saying goes. Leonard made the shot, and the Raptors disposed of the Milwaukee Bucks en route to the team's first NBA Finals berth. The Raps then dethroned the Golden State Warriors, making history in the process: the first title in franchise history and the first team to bring the Larry O'Brien trophy north of the U.S. border.

Meanwhile, in the Western Conference, LeBron and the Lakers hit a speed bump when James sat out 17 games with a groin injury, the longest break of his career. In-fighting on the Golden State Warriors dominated headlines early, but Stephen Curry and his perennial smile-and-shimmy kept the Dubs afloat, and DeMarcus Cousins' appearance in the lineup sparked the reigning champs back into first in the west despite charges from the likes of Portland, Houston and Oklahoma City. None of them could top the Warriors, though. Damian Lillard's showstopper of a series ender in the first round was a highlight seen around the world, but despite Lillard's heroics, Golden State reached the finals for the fifth straight year after easily picking apart the Trail Blazers.

Individually, this season saw milestone after milestone. James Harden obliterated the record books when he scored 57 and 58 on back-to-back nights, without one teammate registering an assist! Russell Westbrook beat Wilt Chamberlain's consecutive triple-double record, finishing with 11, and he joined Wilt the Stilt as the only two humans to put up 20 points, 20 rebounds and 20 assists in one game. Simply incredible. Other players, new kids on the block who are part of a young wave of talented stars, made big strides this season. Denver's Nikola Jokic showed everyone why he is the best passing big man in the league, and his first All-Star nod was the proof in the pudding. The Nuggets spent time atop the standings and made it all the way to Game 7 in the second round of the postseason. Rising stars Luka Doncic, Ben Simmons, Jayson Tatum and Jamal Murray, all featured in this latest edition of *Basketball Now!*, took turns stuffing the stat sheet. New international arrivals now dot the NBA landscape, such as Cameroon's dynamic duo, Joel Embiid and Paskal Siakam. But the NBA is still a league of alpha dogs on alpha teams. Curry, Harden, James, Leonard — these are franchise players dominating the highlight reel, the superstars who are must-watch on Christmas Day or during the All-Star Game.

On the sentimental side, in 2018–19 we said our goodbyes to legends Dirk Nowitzki and Dwyane Wade, who both embarked on a final lap around the league after storied careers and multiple championships. Both are surefire Hall of Famers, generational players for the Miami Heat and the Dallas Mavericks, teams that will now look to restock the cupboard.

The narrative league-wide is probably something you noticed watching even just a game or two: three-point shooting has taken over. Just a few years ago, there was only a handful of teams ahead of the curve that used analytics to win games — meaning fewer midrange twos and more shots from behind the arc. Well, here we are, and almost every team is playing a fast-paced transition game with oodles of raindrops from distance, and the entire league is using advanced in-stadium technology to provide up-to-the-minute statistics. Scoring is way up, which is great for the fans, but that raises a question — is the big man in the middle suddenly a dinosaur? Are we destined for a — gasp — four-point line? Even 7-footers have adapted, and more centers are incorporating the three in their arsenal.

We hope you enjoyed this past NBA season as much as we did, but now that a new season is here, enough looking back. With players changing teams, with franchises on the rise, with superstars destroying the record books, here are the most interesting 50 players in the NBA right now.

James Harden of the Houston Rockets scorched the record books in 2018–19, becoming the first player since Wilt Chamberlain to score back-to-back 55-plus-point games, like he did in January 2019 versus Memphis and Brooklyn.

GIANNIS ANTETOKOUNMPO

MILWA

34

KYRIE IRVING

POSITION POWER FORWARD / SHOOTS RIGHT / HEIGHT 6'11" / WEIGHT 242 LB. / DRAFTED 2013, MILWAUKEE BUCKS, 15TH OVERALL

GIANNIS ANTETOKOUNMPO 34

WHEN YOU'VE GOT a nickname like "the Greek Freak," there's bound to be something special about the way you play. That's exactly the case with Giannis Antetokounmpo, the Milwaukee Bucks star who is tearing up the NBA with an insane combination of length, speed and talent with the ball.

Born to Nigerian parents but raised in Athens, Antetokounmpo grew up poor and hungry, sharing basketball sneakers with his brother Thanasis — the two even hawked souvenirs to tourists to help pay the bills. Giannis, who was scouted at 13, began plying his trade in a low-level second-division Greek league (what one NBA exec deemed "YMCA level") before reaching the pinnacle of basketball. Given his visibility on YouTube it may feel like the 6-foot-11 power forward has been in the NBA for years, but 2018–19 was only the sixth full season for the 15th overall pick of the 2013 draft.

The excitable international star recorded his first career double-double several months into his rookie year, going 16 and 10 against the Brooklyn Nets. By January, he was regularly putting up double-digit figures in points, and his minutes were dramatically increasing, a great sign for a rookie who clearly was picking up on the finer points of the game. Instead of getting buried on the bench, Antetokounmpo was playing 25 to 30 minutes a night for a young Bucks squad focused on creating a winner. For many fans, their first large-scale introduction to the high-flying Greek was at the 2015 Slam Dunk Contest. The Freak walked out into Madison Square Garden with a procession of flower-haired women and the Greek flag draped over his shoulders — not a shabby entrance. But the competition quickly showed that Antetokounmpo's in-game dunks are more exciting than the uncontested jams thrown down in exhibition.

When it comes to games that count, Antetokounmpo's crafty Eurostep move — sometimes started beyond the free-throw line — allows him to get to the basket

'em, 7, blocks against the Charlotte Hornets on the final day of 2016. He may not shoot the three consistently yet — a must for big men these days — but those skills will come once he develops the fundamentals needed to play in the NBA at a high level. And that's happening — in March 2019, Antetokounmpo dropped a career-high 52 points in a win against the Philadelphia 76ers, establishing himself as the go-to offensive weapon up front.

The Bucks made the playoffs in 2016–17, 2017–18 and 2018–19 and are building a nucleus around the Greek prodigy. Antetokounmpo's per-game line in those three seasons was a mind-blowing 25.7 points, 10.4 rebounds, 5.4 assists, 1.6 blocks and 1.5 steals. He plays several positions on the court, giving the Bucks a lot of looks depending on their lineup, and is already one of the NBA's next great superstars.

The Greek Freak had a breakthrough season in 2018–19, establishing himself as a top-five player and an MVP winner. Antetokounmpo made the game look easy, embarrassing opponents with a skill set rarely if ever seen in the NBA — speed, power, athleticism and a two-step move to the basket from the top of the key that makes top defenders look silly. He's become a must-watch household name with moves that defy gravity, and he has effectively changed the fortune of the Bucks franchise, launching Milwaukee into the top spot in the Eastern Conference. The team made the east finals thanks to their frontcourt leader, who dropped 41 versus Detroit in the first round and demolished Boston in Game 4 of the second round, recording 39 points and 16 rebounds on 15 of 22 shooting.

Given enough time, Antetokounmpo may launch himself into the conversation as one of the best international players in the history of the game, alongside stalwarts Dirk Nowitzki and Tim Duncan. He's certain to be the best basketball product to ever come out of the tiny nation of Greece — a once-in-a-generation talent who seems poised to take the basketball world by storm.

midflight. Although he wasn't a rebounding machine in his first few seasons, he's proven that he's certainly capable of getting up on the glass and helping out, as evidenced by the 12.5 boards he averaged in 2018–19. He can also be a help defender by launching in the air against smaller players, and he's added a career 1.3 blocks per game to his arsenal, including 4 stuffs against the Indiana Pacers early in 2015 and 7, count

quickly and slam on surprised players. His length is nearly impossible to guard, his wingspan stretching like a bird of prey in

POSITION POINT GUARD / **SHOOTS** RIGHT / **HEIGHT** 6'3" / **WEIGHT** 190 LB. / **DRAFTED** 2009, GOLDEN STATE WARRIORS, 7TH OVERALL

STEPHEN CURRY 30

HIS SHOT IS as pure as they come, a sweet stroke that finds nothing but net from whatever corner of the earth he hoists it. Stephen Curry was born to shoot basketballs. Whether it be a full-speed breakout-to-pull-up three or a slash to the hoop, he's graceful and almost effortless. Mostly, Steph Curry is a star.

Born Wardell Stephen Curry II in 1988, the point guard comes from basketball pedigree, the son of former NBA player Dell Curry. Dell finished his career in Toronto, where his oldest son Steph spent time playing 1-on-1 in shootarounds with Vince Carter and Tracy McGrady before his undeniable talent led him to star for Davidson College, one of the smallest schools in the NCAA I division.

His arrival put the school on the map, and in Curry's first appearance in the NCAA tournament, he dropped 30 points in a loss to fourth-seeded Maryland. The following year, Curry scored 40 against seventh-seeded Gonzaga. The Wildcats then rattled off victories against second-seeded Georgetown and third-seeded Wisconsin before bowing out to the eventual champion, Kansas. Davidson's magical run was over, but Curry had emerged as one to watch. He averaged 28.6 points per game his final year of college before entering the 2009 NBA Draft, where he was selected seventh overall by the Golden State Warriors.

Listed at 6-foot-3, Curry's simply the most dynamic point guard in the game. He already holds three of the top four spots in the NBA record books for most threes made in one season (402, 2015–16; 324, 2016–17; 286, 2014–15) and sports a career 43 percent mark from downtown while maintaining a 90 percent free-throw percentage.

There's something special about the way he does it all. Aside from the silky smooth release, his basketball IQ is through the roof. One minute he's running the floor off a steal and dunking with authority; the next he's settling the offense down and dishing no-lookers to a trailing teammate. His bag of tricks includes a killer crossover, a spot-up three, circus shots that seem impossible

and a behind-the-back pass that is difficult to intercept.

In 2014–15, he destroyed the competition en route to an NBA Finals berth and his first league MVP win. Curry did it all, hitting miraculous game-winning shots from the corner, dancing his way to the rim and dropping 30-plus with regularity —including 37 in Game 5 of the finals. The Warriors captured the 2015 NBA championship, their first in 40 years, and Curry set a playoff record for most threes with 98, which his fellow Splash Brother, Klay Thompson, tied in 2016.

In 2015–16, Curry won his second regular-season MVP award by a unanimous vote and gained entry into the vaunted 50-40-90 club, but he spent most of the 2016 playoffs hurt. The Warriors still returned to the finals but blew the chance to repeat against the Cleveland Cavaliers. Golden State added Kevin Durant in the off-season, and the presence of two MVPs on the same team ensured the Warriors dominated the Western Conference in 2016–17.

During the 2017 playoffs, Curry displayed his magic once again. He scored 40 points in Game 1 of the Western Conference finals, hitting seven threes. In Game 2 of the NBA Finals against Cleveland, the point guard notched his first-ever postseason triple-double, recording 32 points, 10 rebounds and 11 assists. The Warriors won their second championship in three years, defeating the Cavs in five. Curry dropped 34 points and 10 assists in the deciding game. After notching his third championship and defeating the Cavs for the second straight season in 2018, Curry waved his magic wand again in 2018–19. He scored 51 points in just three quarters in October versus Washington. He regularly hit double digits in made threes and continued his assault on the record books, grabbing third place all-time for three-point shots made. The biggest surprise of the season came when he put in contact lenses for the first time, suggesting the NBA's greatest shooter didn't even have perfect vision as he sank trey after trey.

Perhaps no single game encapsulates Curry more than Game 6 against the

CAREER HIGHLIGHTS

- Named NBA MVP two times (2014–15, 2015–16)
- Has played in six All-Star Games (2014–19)
- Was the NBA scoring champion in 2015–16
- Set the NBA record for three-pointers in a single season (402) in 2015–16
- Ranks first in career three-point field goal percentage (.436) among active NBA players

Houston Rockets in round two of the 2019 playoffs. With Houston facing elimination, Curry had zero points at the half. Like a fighter jet he then exploded for 33 points, winning the series and sending Golden State's bitter rival packing. Curry, playing with a dislocated finger on his nonshooting hand, called it "the best 18 minutes of my career." The Warriors made it to their fifth NBA Finals — all thanks to one of the best point guards the world has ever seen.

POSITION POWER FORWARD–CENTER / **SHOOTS** RIGHT / **HEIGHT** 6'10" / **WEIGHT** 253 LB. / **DRAFTED** 2012, NEW ORLEANS HORNETS, 1ST OVERALL

ANTHONY DAVIS [3]

A NEW SUPERSTAR has emerged in the NBA. He's tall, he's long and he sports the league's most recognizable unibrow. At 6-foot-11 and 253 pounds, Anthony Davis is one of the most talked-about forwards in the league. If he keeps it up, we may be watching a future MVP at work.

The Chicago kid jumped from high school to the University of Kentucky, where he led the Wildcats to a national championship as a freshman in 2012 over the Kansas Jayhawks. Davis was named MVP of that game after recording 6 points, 16 rebounds, 5 assists, 6 blocks and 3 steals. Former U of K coach Tubby Smith said after the game, "He may be the best player to [ever] play at Kentucky."

His inclusion as a teenager on the 2012 U.S. men's Olympic team signaled he deserved to be mentioned among the elite. At the time, LeBron James said that Davis reminded him of four-time NBA blocks leader Marcus Camby. Kobe Bryant resolved to mentor the 19-year-old after seeing him finish alley-oops from Kevin Durant and Chris Paul. His length, defensive awareness and energy impressed the group of future Hall of Famers.

In his first full season playing for the New Orleans Hornets (2012–13), Davis played 64 games, averaging 13.5 points per game, 8.2 rebounds and 1.8 blocks despite several injury scares. He managed to impress league-wide, posting 28 points and 11 rebounds versus Milwaukee early in the season and consistently dropping double-doubles in the second half.

The following year the team name changed to the Pelicans, and it proved positive. Davis saw his totals increase, nearly doubling his trips to the line and increasing his free-throw percentage to .791 — impressive for a big man. He finished with 20.8 points per game, 10 rebounds and 2.8 blocks in 67 games.

His 2014–15 NBA campaign got off to a blistering start. He dropped an opening night for the ages: 26 points, 17 rebounds, 9 blocks, 3 steals and 2 assists — results

not seen since the likes of another big man, Hakeem Olajuwon. Davis continually drove defenses mad with his ruthless combo of size and touch. At the end of January, he was on pace for the greatest player efficiency rating (PER) in the history of the NBA. He finished with a mark of 30.81. The only two players since 1973–74 (when the NBA began tracking individual turnovers) to have posted higher ratings? Michael Jordan and LeBron James.

If he's not making a deft post move, Davis is hitting nothing but net from 15 feet out. He can dribble like a guard or drop back for a three and run the court with elegance and power. And of course, there's that 7-foot-5 wingspan.

His offensive output in 2015–16 was equally devastating, despite his missing 14 games — he finished the season with 24.3 points and 10.3 assists. He matched Shaquille O'Neal and Chris Webber as the only NBA players since 1983 to post a 50-point, 20-rebound game: he went off for 59 and 22 versus Detroit in February 2016,

establishing a new franchise record for points scored in a game.

His opening game of 2016–17 was nothing short of miraculous — 50 points, 16 rebounds and 7 steals. Later in the season, he went off for 46 points and 21 rebounds versus Charlotte. He continued dominating opponents and increased his season totals to 28 points a night — including 11.8 off the glass — 2.2 blocks and an 80 percent free-throw percentage. In 2017–18, Davis scored 40 points eight times, went off for a staggering 53 and 18 against the lowly Phoenix Suns and put up 10 blocks versus the Utah Jazz. When an Achilles injury forced the recently acquired DeMarcus Cousins to the sidelines, Davis took over. He led the Pelicans to a sweep of the Portland Trail Blazers in the first round.

Things were looking bright, but in 2018–19 the Pelicans took a dip in the standings after their strong playoff run. At the end of January, Davis shook up the NBA by announcing he had no intention of signing another long-term contract

with the Pelicans and that he wanted to be traded. Since his announcement, rumors began to swirl about his desire to team up with LeBron James in Los Angeles, which is exactly what happened in the 2019 off-season.

Now a member of the LA Lakers, Davis embarks on a new chapter of his career alongside the greatest player of the modern generation. Will Davis become the Shaq to James' Kobe? Only time will tell, but it's an exciting time to be Davis as he embarks on rebuilding the struggling Lakers into a contender in the west.

CAREER HIGHLIGHTS

- Named to NBA All-Rookie (First Team) in 2012–13
- Named All-Star Game MVP in 2017
- Has played in six All-Star Games (2014–2019)
- Named to All-NBA First Team three times (2014–15, 2016–17, 2017–18)
- Led the league in blocks per game in 2013–14 (2.8), 2014–15 (2.9) and 2017–18 (2.6)

BROOKLYN NETS

POSITION SMALL FORWARD / **SHOOTS** RIGHT / **HEIGHT** 6'9" / **WEIGHT** 240 LB. / **DRAFTED** 2007, SEATTLE SUPERSONICS, 2ND OVERALL

KEVIN DURANT 7

PURE, UNADULTERATED TALENT. That's what you see when watching Kevin Durant play. He oozes talent and flashes brilliance, which have made him into one of the great heirs to the modern basketball throne.

Durant grew up on the outskirts of Washington, D.C., where his mother worked long shifts hauling 70-pound mailbags for the postal service. Gangly, he entered an elementary school gym and quickly learned the game under the supervision of a life-changing mentor nicknamed Chucky, who was shot to death when Durant was in high school. To honor his mentor, the future NBA superstar chose to wear the number 35 for most of his career, Chucky's age when he died. Chucky's death hardened the shy Durant, and he immersed himself in basketball.

He played one season at the University of Texas at Austin, averaging 25.8 points, and was drafted to the NBA second overall in 2007 behind Greg Oden. The Seattle SuperSonics won only 20 games with their fresh draft choice in the backcourt. Durant was skinny, shot the ball too much and had a poor diet. His game appeared one-dimensional, and he was nicknamed "Starvin' Marvin." But when the team moved to Oklahoma in 2008–09 everything changed. Durant was always in the gym, always shooting, always leading by example. Despite a 3-29 start, Oklahoma won 20 of their last 30, and change was in the air. In 2009–10, Durant won the scoring title at

21 years of age, the youngest ever to do so. He continued dominating the league, leading Oklahoma to the Western Conference finals in 2011 and the NBA Finals in 2012.

Durant scorched the NBA for a career-high 32 points per game, 7.4 rebounds and 5.5 assists during his MVP season in 2013–14, punctuated by his heart-wrenching acceptance speech where he thanked his mom by saying, "You're the real MVP."

After a season largely lost because of chronic foot problems, Durant once again led his squad all the way to Game 7 of the

- Named NBA MVP for 2013–14
- Named NBA Finals MVP two times (2017, 2018)
- Named NBA Rookie of the Year for 2007–08
- Named All-Star Game MVP two times (2012, 2019)
- Named to All-NBA First Team six times (2009–10 to 2013–14, 2017–18)

dominated in the 68 games he played, averaging 26.4 points and 6.8 boards per contest. More importantly, he led the team while Curry was injured, especially in the first round of the playoffs. The true test came when Golden State faced Houston in the Western Conference finals. Durant dropped 34 in Game 7, and he would keep it going as the Warriors swept the Cavs in the finals. He was named MVP for the second straight playoffs, posting 29 points, 7.8 rebounds and 4.7 assists en route to the championship.

In 2018–19, Durant was under a microscope: a heated exchange early in the season with teammate Draymond Green led some to question the chemistry of the team. Despite the speculation, the team still finished first in the Western Conference, and the Warriors made the finals for a fifth straight year. Durant was unstoppable in the first two rounds before a calf injury side-lined him; he averaged over 34 points per game and looked the part of the best player in the league.

Durant ruptured his Achilles in the 2019 finals and is set for a long rehab period, now with the Brooklyn Nets, with whom he signed a four-year, $164 million deal. But make no mistake, when he returns, Durant will still be the purest, most natural scorer in the NBA. No one doubts the talent. No one doubts the numbers. And now with several championship titles, Durant may finally have entered the conversation as one of the greatest players of his generation.

2016 Western Conference finals. In Game 6 in Oklahoma, Durant was just five minutes away from a second berth in the NBA Finals when Golden State Warrior sharpshooter Klay Thompson hit 11 three-pointers and cued a fourth-quarter comeback that signaled Durant's final home game for the franchise that drafted him.

Everyone, including Durant, knew he needed to start winning championships to secure his legacy. Sensing Oklahoma had peaked, he elected to join the Warriors as a free agent in 2016–17. Durant averaged 25.1 points, 8.3 rebounds and 4.8 dimes over the regular season despite missing 20 games with a knee injury. He and Steph Curry formed a one-two punch that proved

nearly impossible to match as the Warriors lost just once down the stretch and once in the postseason.

That playoff run would go a long way to change the minds of Durant's doubters. Durant played some of the best basketball of his career. The forward led all scorers in Game 1 of the NBA Finals with 38 points. The following game, he posted a game-high 33, adding 13 rebounds, 6 assists, 5 blocks and 3 steals — an all-around game that had tongues wagging. He capped off the five-game series with a 39-point performance in Game 5, winning his first championship ring and being named finals MVP.

Durant took less than max money to stay in Golden State in 2017–18 and

POSITION SHOOTING GUARD–POINT GUARD / SHOOTS LEFT / HEIGHT 6'5" / WEIGHT 220 LB. / DRAFTED 2009, OKLAHOMA CITY THUNDER, 3RD OVERALL

JAMES HARDEN 13

JAMES HARDEN IS hard to miss. He's more beard than ball, more flash than pan. Harden's become one of the league's true superstars, and thanks to his myriad skills he's propelling the Houston Rockets to the top of the NBA class.

A myth pervaded that Harden's high school coach, Scott Pera, deemed him an NBA star upon first sight, but in 2012 he said simply that he could tell Harden "was going to be a good high school player." What's unmistakable is the guard had gifts early on, and his Artesia High team won two state championships before he accepted a scholarship to Arizona State.

Taken third by the Oklahoma City Thunder, Harden found himself outside the starting five on a stacked young franchise that included Kevin Durant and Russell Westbrook. The circumstance wasn't one that spelled certain stardom. No matter, Harden made his case as best he could.

In the 2011–12 season, a coming-out year for the bearded wonder, he was named Sixth Man of the Year, the youngest in history. Harden's presence off the bench was a massive factor in the Thunder's reaching the NBA Finals that season. Problem was, after a finals loss to the Miami Heat, there was simply no way Oklahoma could keep Harden as well as future MVPs Durant and Westbrook. Unable to offer Harden the "franchise player" money he deserved heading into the 2012–13 season, the Thunder dealt the talented guard to the Rockets,

where he's become the backbone of the team and the centerpiece for an offense that relies heavily on the three-point shot.

What did Harden do once he got to Houston? He started with a first game for the ages: 37 points, 12 assists, 6 rebounds and 4 steals. He continued his stellar play and made his first All-Star appearance. He posted a 45-point night and his first

triple-double and finished the year as the fifth highest scorer in the NBA (25.9 points per game). And all this after helping Team USA to Olympic gold in 2012.

Harden doesn't just score, he impacts the entire game when he's on the court. Using his lethal Eurostep, the left-handed dribbler drives to the basket, where he's one of the NBA's top players in drawing fouls. (And

it doesn't hurt that he's a career 85 percent free-throw shooter.) He's also patented the step-back three — nearly impossible to defend and looks almost like a travel. It's gained in popularity, and other players around the league are now mimicking Harden's trademark shot.

In 2016–17, Harden started demolishing the record books. That season he put up 22 triple-doubles, which included a never-before-seen 53 points, 17 assists and 16 rebounds versus the Knicks. If not for Russell Westbrook's own onslaught of the record books, Harden would have been a sure lock for MVP.

The arrival of Chris Paul in 2017–18 signaled the Rockets were serious about trying to win, and they made it all the way to the Western Conference finals, falling to the Golden State Warriors in seven games. Harden for his part dominated the league, leading the NBA in scoring (averaging 30.6 points per game) and winning the 2018 MVP Award — a mere prelude to his next campaign.

The 2018–19 season was the stuff of legend. With Paul hurt for a long stretch, Harden took matters into his own hands, entering the history books with a 61-point game versus the Knicks and a 32-game streak of 30 points or more. He surpassed Wilt Chamberlain's second-longest streak, although he still has a ways to go if he wants to top Wilt's record of 65 games. Harden triple-doubled at will, and at one point he scored 263 consecutive points without a teammate's recording an assist. In late February he torched Miami, scoring 58 points, 10 assists and 7 boards while going a perfect 18 of 18 from the line. He averaged a mind-boggling 36.1 points — which surpassed Kobe Bryant's 2005–06 average — and 7.5 assists, becoming the first player ever to average 35-plus points per game and 7-plus assists. Quite simply, it's been one of the most dominant seasons in the modern era. Yet he still couldn't breach the wall of Golden State Warriors who stood in the way of his first NBA title, despite averaging 35 points a game in the second round.

In the 2019 off-season, Paul was traded

to the Thunder in exchange for Harden's former teammate and 2016–17 MVP Westbrook. But the question remains: will Harden and Westbrook's combined offensive prowess be enough to topple the powerhouse teams of the Western Conference?

In just a few years the gregarious guard, whose beard has its own Twitter account, has become one of the best players in the world, and if he helps bring a championship to Houston, he'll live on with Rockets legends like Moses Malone and Hakeem Olajuwon.

CAREER HIGHLIGHTS

- Named NBA MVP in 2017–18
- Has played in seven All-Star Games (2013–2019)
- Named to All-NBA First Team five times (2013–14, 2014–15, 2016–17 to 2018–19)
- Led the NBA in points per game two times (2017–18, 2018–19)
- Won an Olympic gold medal with the U.S. men's basketball team in London in 2012

POSITION POINT GUARD / **SHOOTS** RIGHT / **HEIGHT** 6'3" / **WEIGHT** 193 LB. / **DRAFTED** 2011, CLEVELAND CAVALIERS, 1ST OVERALL

KYRIE IRVING  11

THE TALENT IS there. The personality is too. What Kyrie Irving needed to become one of the greatest stars in the NBA was to take the always-elusive next step. And after the point guard dropped two 50-point games in 2014–15, it was the first sign he'd finally arrived. It was also the precursor to his game-winning shot in Game 7 of the 2016 NBA Finals that awarded the city of Cleveland its first professional sports championship in 52 years.

Irving was born in Melbourne, Australia, and raised in New Jersey. His father played professionally Down Under before relocating to the Garden State, where the younger Irving flourished. He owes a lot to his father, who failed to make the NBA but ensured his son would. Irving, who was dribbling a ball at just 13 months old, wrote himself a note in fourth grade that said "GOAL: PLAY IN THE NBA."

He went to Duke, where he played just 11 games his first season because of a toe injury. Even with the limited college trial, everyone knew of the talented guard. In a classic case of one-and-done, Irving declared for the draft and was selected first overall by the Cleveland Cavaliers. In his rookie season he averaged 18.5 points per game, 5.4 assists and a shooting percentage of .469 en route to Rookie of the Year honors despite missing 15 games. But playing for a hapless 21-45 Cavs team wasn't ideal for the rising star, who garnered attention as the 2014 All-Star Game MVP.

Irving hit the jackpot with the return of LeBron James to Cleveland to start 2014–15. Irving's career averages saw only a slight uptick with James in the mix, but with the explosive forward gobbling up the majority of attention from defenders, Irving was given time to shine in ways he hadn't before. He became the Cavs' driving force, the

straw that stirred the drink. Take the night that Irving, with LeBron nursing a wrist injury, stung the talent-heavy Portland Trail Blazers for 55 points in a 99–94 win. Irving sunk 11 three-pointers and went a perfect 10 for 10 from the stripe. Not to be outdone by even himself, the point guard upped the ante and sent a message to the entire league

of the NBA Finals, despite a knee injury to Irving in Game 1. Irving averaged 19 points, 3.8 assists and 3.9 rebounds over 13 playoff games and was sorely missed as a three-point threat in the finals. He'd avenge the loss the following season. Finally healthy midway through the year, Irving was primed for playoff basketball after dropping a cool 35 points in the second-to-last game of the season versus Atlanta, his season high. Irving saved his best for the NBA Finals, hitting the game-winning three-point dagger that toppled the Golden State Warriors in the final minute of Game 7. It's become Irving's signature highlight, delivering the Cavaliers their first NBA championship.

In 2016–17 Irving was a horse, averaging 25 points per game, nearly 6 dimes, 90 percent from the stripe and 40 percent from beyond the arc. The Cavs made it to the Finals again for a rematch against the Warriors, but this time they would lose in five.

Then it all blew up, and Irving was traded to the Boston Celtics for 2017–18. His first season in Beantown started strong — the new alpha dog led his team to 16 straight wins. But a late-season injury meant no postseason play for the point guard. In 2018–19, a rejuvenated Irving willed his young teammates to rise to the challenge, but growing pains crept in despite herculean efforts from their on-court leader. The Celtics, favorites at the beginning of the season to top the conference, finished fourth in the east. Irving's numbers were good — 23.8 points, 5 rebounds and nearly 7 assists — but the Celtics were ousted in the second round of the playoffs by the Milwaukee Bucks, and Irving struggled at times to find his shot. In the 2019 off-season he signed a four-year, $142 million deal with the Brooklyn Nets, joining Kevin Durant and DeAndre Jordan in New York.

It's an exciting time to be Irving. He weathered some lean years in Cleveland to begin his career, got his dues in the form of a ring, and now, paired with one of the best ballers on the planet, is charged with leading a new team to the promised land.

CAREER HIGHLIGHTS

- Named NBA Rookie of the Year for 2011–12
- Named All-Star Game MVP in 2014
- Has played in six All-Star Games (2013–2015, 2017–19)
- Won the NBA Three-Point Contest in 2013
- Named to All-NBA Second Team in 2018–19

with his 57-point performance against the reigning-champion San Antonio Spurs. "The kid is special," James said following the game. Charles Barkley called it "one of the best individual performances I've ever seen."

The additions of Kevin Love, Kyle Korver and Tristan Thompson made the Cavs a talent-laden, veteran-heavy team and a contender in the east. The 2014–15 season saw the Cavs make it all the way to Game 6

POSITION POWER FORWARD–SMALL FORWARD / **SHOOTS** RIGHT / **HEIGHT** 6'8" / **WEIGHT** 250 LB. / **DRAFTED** 2003, CLEVELAND CAVALIERS, 1ST OVERALL

LEBRON JAMES 23

FEW BASKETBALL PLAYERS define an era. But when they do, they're often known by a single name. Kareem. Bird. Magic. Jordan. And the man who has ushered basketball into the 21st century is known simply as LeBron.

LeBron James was born in 1984 in Akron, Ohio. By his junior year of high school, he was the most famous teen athlete in the United States, appearing on the cover of *Sports Illustrated* and wowing the nation with his unique blend of size, speed and athleticism. When the Cleveland Cavaliers made him the number one overall pick in the 2003 NBA Draft, he was already more famous than Bird, Magic or Jordan were at that stage in their careers. One writer called James "the most hyped basketball player ever."

Football-player big at 6-foot-8 and 250 pounds, James immediately made an impact on the NBA, dropping 25 points in his first game. James was the automatic choice for Rookie of the Year, and in his second season, LeBron started making magic, scorching the Toronto Raptors for 56 points and posting four games of 40 points or more and 22 games with 30 points or more — astonishing numbers for a 20-year-old.

Despite being the league's leading scorer in 2007–08 with 30 points per game, LeBron bettered himself during the 2008–09 season. He led the Cavs in the five major statistical categories en route to a 66-16 record. But a third-round exit at the hands of the

CAREER HIGHLIGHTS

- Named NBA MVP four times (2008–09, 2009–10, 2011–12, 2012–13)
- Named NBA Finals MVP three times (2012, 2013, 2016)
- Named All-Star Game MVP three times (2006, 2008, 2018)
- Has played in 15 All-Star Games (2005–2019)
- Won an Olympic gold medal with the U.S. men's basketball team in Beijing in 2008 and London in 2012

Orlando Magic ruined hopes of a title to cap off his MVP-winning year. Lack of success in Cleveland weighed on James. Opting out of his contract with Cleveland and signing with the Miami Heat for the 2010–11 season allowed James to form a mini-dynasty with Chris Bosh and Dwyane Wade.

In terms of legacy making, he accomplished his goal, reaching the finals four times in a row during his tenure with the Heat, winning the title twice and being named MVP twice more to go along with the two he earned in Cleveland. But with an opt-out clause, James controlled his own destiny, choosing to return to Ohio in 2014–15 as the prodigal son.

Everyone wondered if the fans would embrace him — they burned his jersey when he first left the city. But success has a funny way of changing things. With Kyrie Irving and Kevin Love as his new right-hand men, LeBron began eyeing the next challenge. In 2015–16 the Cavs fell to the Golden State Warriors in a nail-biting seven-game finals matchup, but

the following year he brought Cleveland its first title in 50-plus years, climbing back from a 3-1 series deficit in a rematch versus Golden State. James was named finals MVP that year and will forever be remembered for "the Block," a full-court chase-down of Andre Iguodala in the final minutes of Game 7 that helped secure the championship.

LeBron is a 15-time All-Star, four-time MVP, three-time finals MVP and three-time Olympic medalist. His career numbers undoubtedly put him in the upper echelon of anyone who has ever played the game of basketball. He cracked the top-five all-time scoring list in 2018–19 and may be the only man on the planet to have a shot at dethroning Kareem Abdul-Jabbar's record. In 2017 he set the all-time playoff scoring record, eclipsing Michael Jordan, and became the first player to average a triple-double in the NBA Finals despite losing to the Warriors in five games. He may not be the purest scorer, strongest rebounder or most efficient playmaker, but the man who has already been to nine NBA Finals may go down as the most complete basketball player the world has ever seen.

After another finals loss to Golden State in 2017–18, LeBron set his sights on Hollywood and destroying the record books. But his first season with the LA Lakers might well be forgotten. The Lakers came out of the gates in great shape, with James putting 51 on the board versus the Heat and the team contending for a playoff spot. But James incurred an ankle injury near Christmas and missed 17 games, the longest layoff of his career. The young group suffered without their superstar, and LeBron missed the playoffs for the first time in a decade.

The world will be watching — can James take a new group to the promised land and further cement his legacy as the captain of the Lakers? Can he surpass the all-time greats in the record books? Knowing King James, he won't abdicate until he's ready.

KAWHI LEONARD [2]

KAWHI LEONARD BARELY registered on the radar when he first entered the league. Since then he's added a top-five finish in the 2017 MVP voting, nods as MVP of the 2014 and 2019 NBA Finals and two Defensive Player of the Year awards to a hearty list of accolades. He's now taken his talents to Los Angeles, where Leonard is poised to dominate the Western Conference at both ends of the court.

He's an unassuming 6-foot-7, if that's even possible. The 15th overall pick in the 2011 draft, Leonard was traded by the Indiana Pacers to San Antonio, where he became a revelation; his being plucked by the Spurs is another moment of talent evaluation by the franchise that paid great dividends.

Leonard's two years at San Diego State were solid, and in his second and final season, he took the Aztecs all the way to the Sweet 16. That season he threw up averages of 15.9 points and 10.6 rebounds. But Leonard hasn't had the easiest route. His father was killed outside the car wash he owned in Compton in 2008 while Kawhi was in high school. Leonard grew up there washing cars and learned a work ethic that transferred to the court. The tragedy instilled a quiet toughness in his personality, and his agent called Leonard "the most dedicated guy I've ever been around."

In 2013–14, en route to his first championship and first finals MVP award, Leonard contributed 12.8 points and 6.2 boards to the Spurs' attack during the regular season. His presence rounded out a formidably deep group intent on proving that age ain't nothin' but a number — with veterans like Tim Duncan, Tony Parker and Manu Ginobili showing the young Leonard how to win. Despite a slow start that saw him net only 9 points in each of the first two games of the finals, he exploded in Game 3 and was golden the rest of the way, averaging 23.7 points and 9.3 rebounds in the last three games of the series as the Spurs closed out the Miami Heat in five.

Where Leonard really excels is in shutting down his opponent's best players — making

long nights out of games for the league's top stars. He's simply too much of everything all at once: he's too big for some, too long for others, too quick for many and too tenacious on and off the ball for most. (His hands are also massive, 11.25 inches from pinkie to thumb, more than 50 percent larger than the average person and reminiscent of Hall of Famer Scottie Pippen.)

In 2015–16 Leonard averaged 21.2 points a game while maintaining his status as the top shutdown defender in the league. The Spurs went 67-15 in Duncan's final season, but it was Leonard, named a starter for the first time in the 2016 All-Star Game, who garnered all the attention.

During the 2016–17 regular season Leonard put up 25.5 per game, shot 88 percent from the line, hit 38 percent from deep and led the Spurs back to the Western Conference finals before an ankle injury sidelined him. The injury effectively dashed San Antonio's hopes of dethroning the Golden State Warriors, who made their third straight NBA Finals appearance. He played just nine games in 2017–18 because of a quad injury dating back to September 2017, and his relationship with the Spurs' front office grew rockier as the season wore on.

Leonard was traded to Toronto in the 2018 off-season in a blockbuster deal that sent Toronto Raptors forward DeMar DeRozan to the southern climes of San Antonio and Leonard to the Great White North. Although he played only 60 regular-season games because of "load management," Leonard immediately turned Toronto into a serious playoff contender in the rising east. How about the 37 he dropped against the Warriors in November? Or the 45 versus the Jazz he threw down on New Year's Day? He finished the season with a career-high 26.6 points, and the Raptors entered the playoffs as the number two seed thanks to their bona fide superstar. Leonard's playoff run was historic, and his second round versus Philadelphia was the stuff of legend. Leonard racked up 243 total points in the series, third all-time behind Kareem Abdul-Jabbar and Michael Jordan. He also hit

the first and only Game 7, series-winning buzzer beater.

Leonard finished his unforgettable run by leading the Raptors to the team's first championship, ousting the Milwaukee Bucks and then slaying the Golden State Warriors in six games. Leonard was named NBA Finals MVP for his herculean efforts — he led all playoff performers in points, rebounds, steals and minutes. But despite bringing the championship north of the border, in the 2019 off-season Leonard — one of the most sought-after free agents — decided to return home to southern California, signing with the Los Angeles Clippers in a

league-rocking deal that also saw the Clips trade for star forward Paul George.

Leonard's only 28 years old, but with the maturity he's gained as a seasoned playoff veteran and his penchant for clutch moments, the rings, now at two, are bound to pile up. Just wait.

CAREER HIGHLIGHTS

- Named NBA Finals MVP two times (2014, 2019)
- Named NBA Defensive Player of the Year two times (2014–15, 2015–16)
- Named to NBA All-Defensive First Team two times (2015, 2016)
- Has played in three All-Star Games (2016, 2017, 2019)
- Named to All-NBA First Team two times (2015–16, 2016–17)

POSITION POINT GUARD / **SHOOTS** RIGHT / **HEIGHT** 6'0" / **WEIGHT** 175 LB. / **DRAFTED** 2005, NEW ORLEANS HORNETS, 4TH OVERALL

CHRIS PAUL  ③

IF YOU WANT a smooth, pure basketball player who makes playing in the NBA look easy, look no further than Chris Paul. Ever since winning Rookie of the Year in 2005–06, there has been no stopping the ascent of the 6-foot guard. He's a team leader whose effusive charm, wide smile and hustle on the court have earned him accolades as one of the most respected players in the league.

Paul was taken fourth overall by the New Orleans Hornets, but it wasn't until his third year (2007–08) that he led the Hornets to the playoffs. That season he exceeded the already high expectations placed on him, leading the NBA in assists (925), assists per game (11.6), steals (217) and steals per game (2.7) while knocking down 21.1 points per contest. His dominance on both ends of the floor had him second in MVP voting to the LA Lakers' Kobe Bryant. New Orleans also won their first playoff series that year, a 4-1 romp over the Dallas Mavericks in which Paul recorded three double-doubles in the series and a triple-double in the final game.

But Paul's time with the Hornets was short-lived. Not wanting to play in the basement, he asked to be dealt. After Commissioner David Stern vetoed his trade to the LA Lakers to join Kobe Bryant — a dream scenario — Paul was shipped to the Clippers. There, he teamed with Blake Griffin to form a duo equally formidable to the Paul–Bryant pipe dream.

Paul's a perennial leader in the assist category, leading the league four times. He's a dish-first point guard who looks for backdoor cuts, trailing big men, or plays off the pick and roll. But don't mistake him for an average shooter — he's lethal with an open-look jumper. Paul is creative off the dribble, possesses a killer crossover and can develop an out-of-this world aerial chemistry with his superstar teammates.

A strong court general — always probing new ways to the basket, posing as a threat

CAREER HIGHLIGHTS

- Named NBA Rookie of the Year for 2005–06
- Has played in nine All-Star Games (2008–2016)
- Named to All-NBA First Team four times (2008, 2012–2014)
- Ranks first in assists per game (9.7) among active NBA players
- Won an Olympic gold medal with the U.S. men's basketball team in Beijing in 2008 and London in 2012

to pass, shoot, lob or penetrate deep into the key — Paul is solid on D too. He has led the league in steals six times, including four straight (2010–11 to 2013–14). He is still arguably one of the best defensive point guards in the NBA, and he continues to put up a couple of steals per contest.

Where Paul's critics slam him is in the postseason. But given his virtuoso performance in Game 7 of the first round of the 2015 playoffs against the San Antonio Spurs, that tune started to change. Fighting

through a hamstring injury, Paul drove to the hoop and hit a last-second off-balance, off-the-glass winner to send the Clips to the next round. It was easily the biggest shot of his career and silenced those who claimed Paul isn't clutch.

He put up 19.5 points and 10 dimes the following season, but ever judged on his postseason success, the year was deemed a disappointment when Paul broke his hand in the first round against Portland and the Clippers exited early. The point guard had some serious stat lines in 2016–17, none greater than his 20 points and 20 assists (and zero turnovers) in a 133–105 win versus New Orleans. In the 2017 playoffs, the Clippers fell to the Utah Jazz in seven games despite Paul's averaging 25 points, 10 assists and 5 rebounds. In June 2017, he was traded to the Houston Rockets for seven players and a 2018 draft pick.

Paul finally reached the Western Conference finals with Houston in 2018, his deepest run to date. He helped knock

off the Jazz with a virtuoso performance in Game 5 of the second round, putting up 41 points, 8 threes, 10 dimes and 7 rebounds. A hamstring injury late in Game 5 of the conference finals versus Golden State would be Paul's and the Rockets' undoing. Another hamstring injury sidelined him for 27 games in 2018–19, but upon return, the point guard posted 23 points and 17 assists as he and James Harden made their push for an NBA championship. Houston fell short at the hands of the Warriors once again, and Paul ended up being dealt to the Oklahoma City Thunder in a seismic deal that saw Russell Westbrook move to Houston. Where Paul settles down has yet to be seen, but whoever nabs him will get a veteran leader with a long list of accolades to his name.

Paul has already cracked the top 10 in all-time assists and will likely go down not only as the greatest point guard of his generation but as one of the best to ever grace the floor. For Paul, only a championship will burnish his legacy further.

POSITION POINT GUARD / **SHOOTS** RIGHT / **HEIGHT** 6'3" / **WEIGHT** 200 LB. / **DRAFTED** 2008, SEATTLE SUPERSONICS, 4TH OVERALL

RUSSELL WESTBROOK[0]

IT WAS HARD to tell what the Oklahoma City Thunder (formerly the Seattle SuperSonics) acquired with the fourth overall pick in the 2008 draft when they selected Russell Westbrook. He didn't shine in high school until his senior year, when he averaged 25.1 points per game and grabbed 8.7 rebounds as a point guard for Leuzinger High School in Long Beach, California. One thing was certain though: he made his basketball teams better. Twice, UCLA made the Final Four with Westbrook in the backcourt, and during his last year before declaring for the NBA Draft he posted 12.7 points, 3.7 rebounds and 4.9 assists. But was that any indicator he would become one of the most feared men in the NBA?

His first coach certainly knew, commenting in 2011, "Russell . . . had a vision at a young age of what he wanted to do and where he wanted to get." His father, Russell Sr., also knew — or at least ensured a strong work ethic that would become the backbone of Westbrook's game, as the protégé would take 500 shots per day and do countless sit-ups and push-ups.

That work ethic continued when he arrived in Oklahoma, joining heralded small forward Kevin Durant to form one of the NBA's best one-two combos. But Westbrook began largely in Durant's shadow. It's no slight — Durant is a former MVP, a four-time scoring champ and a 10-time All-Star — so for Westbrook to become as formidable a force as Durant is incredible.

His rookie season, Westbrook put home a solid 15.1 points per game, along with 4.9 rebounds, 5.3 assists and 1.3 steals. By his third year, he'd increased almost every one of those totals en route to a first All-Star appearance. That season he helped lead the Thunder to their first NBA Finals appearance — losing in five games to the Miami Heat. In 2013–14, Westbrook shone in the playoffs despite Oklahoma's loss in the conference finals to San Antonio. He

13 rebounds and 11 assists, the highest point total for any triple-double in NBA history. Westbrook finished the season with 42 triple-doubles — an NBA record and the signature on his MVP season.

Along came Paul George in 2017, and Westbrook had a new lieutenant by his side. The two made a formidable pair, combining elite defense with offensive prowess, but two early-round exits from the playoffs plagued Oklahoma's stars. In 2018–19 the duo dominated, and Westbrook set the NBA record for most consecutive triple-doubles, surpassing Wilt Chamberlain's record and finishing with a trip-dub in 11 straight games. He capped the season with an unheard-of 20-20-20 line versus the Lakers — he's only the second player in NBA history to ever record 20 points, 20 rebounds and 20 assists in one game and the first in five decades. Westbrook finished with his third consecutive season averaging a triple-double and is the only player in NBA history to accomplish the feat.

During one of the most interesting off-seasons in recent memory — one that already saw George move to the LA Clippers — Westbrook was dealt to the Houston Rockets for Chris Paul and a number of first-round draft picks and pick swaps. Now that Westbrook has been reunited with his old Thunder teammate James Harden, the league will be watching to see if these two former MVPs can launch the Rockets to the next level — NBA supremacy.

absolutely commanded the floor, averaging a whopping 26.7 points, 8.1 rebounds and 7.3 assists during the series.

He's one of the most versatile point guards in the game. He can hurt opposing teams in a variety of ways, whether by attacking the hoop, dropping a 15-footer — his "cotton shot" — or passing to a cutting big man. Although Westbrook may not be a reliable three-point threat, his tough-as-nails defense makes up for his lack of deep scoring.

Westbrook and Durant took Oklahoma all the way to Game 7 of the 2016 conference finals but bowed out to the Warriors.

Westbrook, for his part, posted double digits in assists in six of seven games and contributed 26 points and 11 assists a game over 18 playoff games, a slight improvement on his regular-season numbers.

Durant bolted to Golden State when free agency beckoned, leaving Westbrook to helm the Thunder. Quite simply, the point guard put up the most dominant offensive season in the NBA since 1961–62, when Oscar Robertson averaged a triple-double for the entire season. Westbrook's season average of 31.6 points, 10.4 assists and 10.7 rebounds were out of this world. In a late-season game he notched 57 points,

THE NBA DRAFT

BOOM OR BUST IN '84

In 1984, the Portland Trail Blazers selected Sam Bowie second overall, one spot behind Hakeem "the Dream" Olajuwon and one position ahead of a guard from North Carolina named Michael Jordan. In hindsight, how anyone could pass up the greatest basketball player of all time may seem baffling, almost unconscionable. It's why to this day the 1984 draft is the most scrutinized, perhaps the most famous draft class of all time. That's not because of Jordan — it's because of Bowie.

At the time, Jordan's going third made sense. Guards were not seen as focal points of basketball teams in the 70s and 80s — big men like Bill Walton, Julius Erving and Kareem Abdul-Jabbar were — and players like Jordan and Magic Johnson had yet to make a full impact on the psyche of executives and fans during the 80s. The 1984 draft in many ways became a tipping point for a new NBA.

A series of unusual circumstances sent Bowie — the greatest high school player of his era — to Portland. The Trail Blazers selected

Sam Bowie, left, and Hakeem Olajuwon flank NBA commissioner David Stern following the 1984 draft.

future All-Star Clyde Drexler at the guard position in 1983 — he declared before his senior year to enter the '83 draft — so with no need for another backcourt presence, Portland had set their sights beyond Jordan well before the executives gathered in Madison Square Garden for the '84 draft.

Portland, well aware of Bowie's progress, and unhappy with their center Tom Owens, traded the underperforming big to Indiana in June of 1981 in exchange for Indiana's number one pick in '84. Luckily for Portland, the Pacers finished dead last in the east in 1983–84, positioning the Blazers in what became a two-horse race for a game-changing player with the west's worst team, the Houston Rockets. The fate of both franchises came down to a simple coin toss for the number one pick (the draft lottery didn't begin until 1985).

Houston won the flip, and as they say, the rest is history.

By choosing Olajuwon, Drexler's college teammate in Houston, the Rockets got an immensely talented Nigerian-born center who'd taken his college team to back-to-back NCAA finals. Portland's consolation prize was Bowie. The Trail Blazers' prior success with another pass-heavy big man, Bill Walton, weighed heavily in the minds of management prior to the 1984 draft. They needed a center to complement Drexler, not another guard. So they chose big, passing over Jordan.

The debate still rages: do you take the most talented player in the draft, regardless of position, or do you fill a need? Mind you, if Bowie hadn't been injured in college, redshirted and played an extra fifth year, he might have gone number one in '83, and the whole Jordan fiasco would have been prevented. (Olajuwon also redshirted a year upon arrival in the U.S.) Another NBA-ready center, Patrick Ewing, who defeated Olajuwon in the 1984 NCAA finals, remained for his senior season at Georgetown. Drafted first overall in 1985, imagine how insane a draft with Ewing, Bowie, and Olajuwon would have been. Hindsight is 20/20, but one wonders if Bowie's career trajectory would have been different as well if Drexler hadn't declared early and Ewing hadn't declared late. An even greater urban myth (at least according to Olajuwon's autobiography) persists that Portland nearly traded Drexler and the second overall pick to Houston for Ralph Sampson. Meaning the Rockets would have ended up with Jordan, Drexler and Olajuwon — one of those three played in an NBA Finals every season from 1990 to 1998 with their respective teams.

WHO WAS SAM Bowie, and how did he become the biggest bust of all time? A 7-foot-1 high school phenom from Lebanon, Pennsylvania, Bowie, as a junior, took his team all the way to the state final before losing by one point. In his senior year in 1979 he averaged 28.8 points per game. Few centers his size could run the floor with grace and agility at such a young age; few could pass like a guard and post like a big. Bowie was so legendary in high school, he signed

Sam Bowie of Kentucky hauls down a rebound against Georgetown in the 1984 NCAA tournament.

autographs everywhere he went with the signature "the Million Dollar Kid." His face was plastered on the cover of sports sections across the country, including the cover of *Sports Illustrated*. For a time, it's not an overstatement to say that Bowie was the most famous basketball player on the planet. Four hundred colleges contacted the teenager — he eventually chose the University of Kentucky. But injuries in college caused Bowie to miss nearly two years of basketball after a broken leg was left untreated and never healed properly. By the time he reached the NBA Draft in 1984, moments away from realizing his lifelong dream and cashing in big time, he had buckled under the pressure. In 2012, for an ESPN documentary, Bowie revealed he lied to the Trail Blazers about the pain in his leg prior to the draft. When the Portland medical team tapped on his tibia during a physical, Bowie said, "I can still remember them taking a little mallet, and when they would hit me on my left tibia . . . I would tell 'em, 'I don't feel anything.' But deep down inside, it was hurting." Desperate to achieve his NBA dream, he went on to say he did what anyone would have done in his position, and one can't help but look back tragically at a man hanging on to a fading dream.

Inexplicably, Portland factored into another great draft bust, Greg Oden. Taken first overall by the Trail Blazers in 2007, Oden, who retired in 2016, was injured most of his career and never made an impact for any team. Even worse, the Blazers could have had Kevin Durant that year, an heir apparent to Jordan, and in many ways, Oden/Durant is the mirror image of Bowie/Jordan.

Drafts are funny things. The '84 draft was in fact loaded with talent beyond the top three picks, but it's forever become known for the three major players — Olajuwon, Bowie, Jordan. But future Hall of Famers like Charles Barkley (the fifth overall pick) and John Stockton (selected 16th!) get easily forgotten under the shadow of Jordan and company. Even Sam Perkins and Kevin Willis had long, serviceable NBA careers, providing more ammunition in the argument for deepest draft on record. But the latter two have become footnotes in history. Booms and busts are what make a draft memorable — 1984 just happened to have both.

THE KIDS ARE ALL RIGHT, SOMETIMES

Ask fans to name the 13th pick overall in 1996 and they might be hard-pressed to come up with the name Kobe Bryant. Or two picks later, if you were to ask who was drafted 15th overall, would they be able to recall the greatest Canadian import in the history of the NBA, Steve Nash? That same draft was littered with future stars — Allen Iverson first overall, guards Peja Stojakovic (14th) and Derek Fisher (24th), and centers Jermaine O'Neal (17th) and Zydrunas Ilgauskas (20th). Although '84 may possess a plethora of Hall of Famers and an enticing story, '96 counts itself as one of the greatest drafts simply for the sheer number of men who went on to long, potent careers — and three future MVPs.

Bowie actually posted decent numbers his rookie season in the NBA — 10 points per game, 8.6 rebounds — but another broken leg the following year began a long streak of tibial fractures, this time to his right leg, derailing his once promising career, and the "bust" talk began in earnest. At the same time, Jordan was taking off, en route to championship after championship, dropping 40-plus with regularity while Bowie sat on the sidelines helplessly for more than two years. (Jordan, famously competitive, took distinct pleasure in torching Portland over the years for passing him over.) Bowie finally retired in 1995, averaging 10.9 points per game, 7.5 boards and nearly 2 blocks per contest over his career, not horrible numbers by any means, but for the man drafted before Jordan, for the man who played on two broken legs, those numbers will never be good enough.

Was it something in the water that year? Why do certain draft classes produce an inordinate number of NBA-ready stars? Basketball players enter the league at different points in their high school or college careers and enter the draft at various stages in their development. Some commit to four-year college programs and enter the NBA at 21 years of age, while others, like LeBron James — a man by the time he was able to drive — skip postsecondary schooling altogether and enter the league at just 18. (This ended after the 2005

Philadelphia's Allen Iverson drives past a trio of Toronto Raptors, including rookie Chris Bosh (left), in 2003.

advantage that allows those children to excel through the higher levels of the system.)

The 1996 draft class has been called one of the best of all time, with Bryant, Nash and Iverson all going on to win the MVP award — that's by far the most successful group of individuals out of any class. Future stars such as Stephon Marbury and Ray Allen went fourth and fifth, respectively. One can't help but think what the fate of the two Canadian expansion franchises, Toronto and Vancouver, might have been had they not chosen Marcus Camby and Shareef Abdur-Rahim at two and three in '96. Can you imagine being one of the GMs who passed on Bryant, Nash, Allen and Marbury? Camby and Abdur-Rahim turned out to be serviceable NBA players, but certainly not MVPs or All-Stars.

A legit number one can change a city. The aforementioned Iverson took Philly from joke squad to legit contender, making the NBA Finals in 2001. Kobe, however, became part of Phil Jackson's next big thing. His long-term consistency would have made any team better, but perhaps the hardest thing to gauge beyond talent is whether an 18- or 19-year-old has the mental fortitude, stamina and leadership skills to keep winning at a high level. For all the Bryants out of high school, there is a Jonathan Bender (fifth overall, Toronto, 1999), Darius Miles (third overall, LA Clippers, 2000) and DeSagana Diop (eighth overall, Cleveland, 2001) — all of them massive mistakes that have haunted those GMs for years.

For all the research, talent assessment, scouting and hand-wringing that go into drafting, how do so many teams get it wrong? Is it really just luck of the draw? This is what New Jersey Nets coach John Calipari (now head coach of Kentucky) said on draft night in 1996: "We really like Kobe. I think he's gonna be a terrific player in the NBA. But for us, right now, where we are and what we needed, I think in the end, [the right choice] was Kerry Kittles."

His is a common refrain: despite obviously talented players, teams often draft on need, not talent (or at least they used to). The Nets needed a forward that year, not a guard — similar to the Blazers in '84.

In 1996, Philadelphia 76ers GM Brad Greenberg, who had the first overall pick, said at the time that he didn't want a teenager. "I wasn't

draft, when the league mandated that a player must turn 19 no later than December 31 of the year of the draft and be at least one year removed from high school graduation.)

A common refrain nowadays is "one-and-dones," players who possess the physical talent to play in the NBA at just 19 years of age and suit up for just one year of college. The 2014 first overall pick — and subsequent 2015 Rookie of the Year — Andrew Wiggins, did just that. He played one year at Kansas, a school dedicated to shaping one-and-dones, before upgrading to the NBA. If not for the rule change, he may have been a high school declarant.

There's no magic potion for why '96 or '84 exists, no Malcolm Gladwell moment to fall back on. (Gladwell argues that for hockey players, month of birth determines future success for NHLers because at certain age levels, kids are grouped together by birth year, and an inordinate number of NHL players are born in the first six months of the year, and being older/faster/stronger at 12 or 13 is an

Carmelo Anthony, left, Dwyane Wade, center, and Chris Bosh make a media appearance prior to the 2003 NBA Draft. The trio were respectively selected third, fifth and fourth.

comfortable going with a [high school] kid for the number one pick vs. Iverson." In hindsight, despite Iverson's brilliance, he chose wrong when you consider the longevity of Bryant's career and what he meant to the Lakers. Iverson ended up doing wonders revitalizing the Philly basketball market, but he flamed out before winning anything substantial. Bryant went on to five rings. In the end, the 76ers missed out on a once-in-a-generation talent and a future Hall of Famer, but would they have done it differently?

It's important to remember that drafting an 18-year-old out of high school in the mid-90s was less common and ultimately seen as a gamble. When Minnesota took a teenaged Kevin Garnett fifth overall in 1995, it was seen as backwards thinking rather than as trendsetting.

Garnett proved his naysayers wrong and went on to have a spectacular career, but one without a championship for Minnesota. Yet he paved the way for Dwight Howard, LeBron and other high schoolers who made the jump to the Association.

FAST-FORWARD TO 2003 — a draft that rivals '96 and '84 in talent level. The draft had an immediate short-term talent impact on the NBA as well as a long-term one that would change the course of the NBA landscape, specifically in how teams are built and how teams win championships. Number one that year was a gimme. LeBron James was as automatic as they come, the greatest high schooler ever, a football player's build in a basketball player's body, and the hope was he would be a franchise changer for his hometown of Cleveland. Next pick — the only misstep of the top five — was Darko Milicic. The following three — Carmelo Anthony, Chris Bosh and Dwyane Wade — became Olympians and All-Stars, and for Bosh, Wade and James, future champions with the Miami Heat twice over. It's the best

Derrick Rose playing in 2014. Chicago, who chose Rose first overall in 2008, had a 1.7 percent chance of winning the first pick at that year's draft. If the odds held up, Chicago would have wound up with the ninth overall pick in 2008.

top five ever seen, even inclusive of Milicic, and surely better than Jordan's draft year.

But more important is what happened later in their careers. When James and Bosh both opted out of their contracts to join Wade in 2010, a new era began in the NBA, one where players were suddenly mindful of taking control of their own destiny in a salary cap era. It was the ultimate recognition that no one individual can win a ring. James applied the same approach to team building when he rejoined the Cavaliers in 2014, opting out of his contract in Miami to sign with Cleveland. He was instrumental in convincing the brass to trade their number one pick, Canadian Andrew Wiggins, for Kevin Love. Along with point guard Kyrie Irving, the new trio formed a formidable threat and, in 2015–16, delivered the first championship to fans in Ohio in over 50 years.

GAMBLING IN THE LOTTERY ERA

For the first 20 years of the NBA Draft, beginning in 1964, a coin flip decided where a first pick landed. That flip could determine how a franchise might flourish or perish. Heads or tails. Pure luck. A 50/50 chance. But finally, in 1984, the NBA Board of Governors voted to introduce the lottery, a weighted system that gave the worst team in the NBA the greatest chance of securing the number one pick. The league has never looked back, and never has the marriage between ping-pong and basketball been so important to sport.

Fourteen numbered balls — one to fourteen — are stuffed in a drum. One thousand and one combinations exist, and each team in the lottery is assigned a four-number combo. To determine the draft order, four numbers are sucked up through the pipes. Whatever team has that combination wins the pick. The balls are returned, the process is repeated, and since then, the commissioner's familiar refrain can be heard through the rafters of the host city every June. "With the first pick in the NBA Draft, the [LUCKY TEAM NAME] selects . . ."

But beyond the obvious number ones that have emerged over the years, GMs are shifting away from drafting positionally and focusing on talent, especially overseas. Draft picks are inherently calculated gambles — small point guard and two-time MVP Steph Curry was taken seventh overall by Golden State — but sometimes they are just total freakin' long shots. Take Bruno Caboclo, the Toronto Raptors' 20th pick in 2014. Few had heard of him outside of a handful of NBA scouts and general managers. Projected to go second round, his selection was immediately questioned on social media. Who was this guy? Why would the Raptors blow their first-rounder on such an obscure kid? But then-GM Masai Ujiri saw something in Caboclo. Long on potential — he has an enormous 7-foot-6 wingspan — the raw rookie represents exactly the type of risk teams are willing to make in a growing international market. Teams aren't focused on

drafting a big man like they were in the 80s with Bowie. Size, speed, long arms for defense and a predilection for hitting threes are all more important than a big body in the middle. And with the success of the Spurs — drafting an unknown commodity such as Tony Parker from Europe — teams are more comfortable taking risks with international players, particularly if it doesn't cost them salary while they hone their skills in European basketball leagues. Additionally, there's more parity in talent level than ever before.

Former Cleveland Cavaliers GM David Griffin said at the 2014 draft: "I don't think there's a clear cut number one pick in most drafts. I think when people say that, they have a really strong feeling

for one player over another, but there's not necessarily a consensus." The same might be said for lower picks like Caboclo. Ujiri, perhaps worried another general manager would snap up his guy before the second round, weighed the risk and deemed it acceptable. He and the Raptors were then free to develop the player as they saw fit. The reality is most picks don't pan out anyway, and it's likely Caboclo may not be a productive NBA player — he was a reserve on the team and played most of his minutes in the G League. Caboclo was eventually traded and finally found minutes on a rebuilding Memphis Grizzlies team. But if he becomes a future star . . . boom. Ujiri looks like a genius.

BOOMS AND BUSTS. That's what sticks in the minds of many as they look back on the greatest drafts in the history of the league. For every Michael Jordan, there's a Sam Bowie. Taken before the greatest basketball player to ever live, Bowie became an unfortunate punch line, a player who could never live up to expectations. Perhaps history has been unkind to him. Or maybe for every Jordan, there are a thousand Sam Bowies, a thousand hopefuls who dream of NBA stardom. The hope and the dream of every NBA executive is choosing the right one.

DAMIAN LILLARD

POSITION SHOOTING GUARD–SMALL FORWARD / **SHOOTS** RIGHT / **HEIGHT** 6'8" / **WEIGHT** 232 LB. / **DRAFTED** 2011, CHICAGO BULLS, 30TH OVERALL

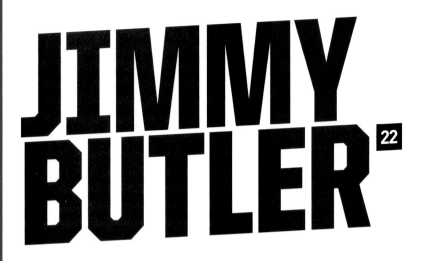

JIMMY BUTLER 22

AT 6-FOOT-7 AND 232 pounds, with guard skills and big size, Jimmy Butler is part of an emerging class of NBA stars who can play multiple roles and who bring a different, exciting blend of athleticism to the NBA. Between 2011–12 and 2016–17 Butler was the face of the Chicago Bulls franchise. And after veteran Dwyane Wade mentored the shooting guard in 2016–17, Butler now seems braced to take the leap to superstardom.

Butler's backstory is one of perseverance and overcoming a stacked deck. Abandoned by his father at birth and kicked out of the house by his mother at 13, Butler could have easily slipped through the cracks. But he ultimately persevered, living with a friend's family in the outskirts of Houston in a town called Tomball. With talent that was off the charts and an incredible drive to learn, Butler averaged nearly 20 points and 9 rebounds a game during his senior year of high school. In 2017, Tomball High raised his No. 1 jersey to the rafters.

Butler was a slow but steady worker — he was ranked just 73rd in the entire state of Texas before jumping from high school to junior college ball. He excelled and moved up to NCAA Division I school Marquette University after Marquette's coach noticed him while scouting another player at Butler's junior college. He played three years at Marquette, averaging 15.7 points in his final season under coach Buzz Williams, a tough-nosed drill sergeant whom Butler credits for instilling in him a tenacious work ethic and never-stop attitude. But even when Butler's stock rose after his promising stint at Marquette, he still was unheralded coming out of college, taken 30th overall by Chicago in the 2011 draft.

In January 2013 he made a big impression on Bulls teammates and fans alike

CAREER HIGHLIGHTS

- Named NBA Most Improved Player for 2014–15
- Named to NBA All-Defensive Second Team four times (2013–14 to 2017–18)
- Has played in four All-Star Games (2015–2018)
- Named to All-NBA Third Team two times (2016–17, 2017–18)
- Won an Olympic gold medal with the U.S. men's basketball team in Rio in 2016

after his strong defense held the legendary Kobe Bryant to just 7 of 22 from the field, acquiring the nickname "Kobe Stopper" as he strutted off the court. Butler continued impressing his colleagues on the defensive end, facing up against LeBron James in the playoffs and cementing a rep as one of the few men in the league who can limit King James' numbers. In early 2014 Butler played 60 minutes in a triple OT thriller versus the Orlando Magic, the most minutes in Bulls history and tied for eighth most of all time.

In 2016–17 Butler easily eclipsed his previous points totals, finishing the season with 23.9 points per game and becoming the go-to guy in the Bulls' offensive scheme. He put the first punctuation mark on the power

transfer just after Christmas when he hit the game-winning shot versus the Brooklyn Nets to finish with 40 on the night. The play the coach drew up? "Give the ball to Jimmy." It was a game in which Wade left with a migraine and Butler took over. It wouldn't be the last time. He dropped two clutch late-game free throws for a win versus the Boston Celtics right before the All-Star break, and he registered his first triple-double of the season against a LeBron-less Cleveland Cavaliers team in late February, posting a line of 18 points, 10 boards and 10 helpers.

In June 2017 Butler was traded to the Minnesota Timberwolves in a deal that saw Zach LaVine, Kris Dunn and 7th overall

pick Lauri Markkanen move into the Bulls' locker room. Butler made an impact in his short time in Minnesota, averaging 22.2 points and 5.3 rebounds a night, and the T-wolves nearly missed the 2018 playoffs after he was sidelined with an injury for 17 games. The young squad was ousted by Houston in the first round of the playoffs, and Butler seemed increasingly unhappy with the situation in Minnesota. He was traded again at the beginning of 2018–19 after a spirited preseason practice saw him call out the Timberwolves organization's work ethic. He took that no-nonsense mentality to Philadelphia, where he hit two game-winning shots in his first eight games and instilled a veteran presence on a young, up-and-coming team. Butler helped lead the 76ers to Game 7 of round two, only to lose the series to Kawhi Leonard's series-ending buzzer beater. Butler, for his part, played monster minutes and scored big bucket after big bucket, earning his rep as a clutch player.

Butler's attitude and will to win are a deadly combination, and after he signed a four-year, $142 million deal with the Miami Heat, fans in Florida should be salivating over the potential to go deep into the playoffs with him in their frontcourt. The only question left is can he bring Larry O'Brien back to South Beach?

POSITION CENTER / **SHOOTS** RIGHT / **HEIGHT** 6'11" / **WEIGHT** 270 LB. / **DRAFTED** 2010, SACRAMENTO KINGS, 5TH OVERALL

DEMARCUS COUSINS 15

WHEN YOU'RE 6-FOOT-6 in eighth grade, certain things seem likely. For instance, if you have a single athletic bone in your body, and you don't mind hitting people, chances are you'll find yourself on a football field. That is exactly where DeMarcus Cousins found himself as a youth. Just as likely was that Cousins would be a shoo-in to rule the basketball court. Yet, at 14 he'd never really played. Destiny, however, has a way of carving a path. After a chance encounter with an AAU recruiter, who thought the eighth grader was a high school senior, Cousins got his basketball start. The following year, he dominated older, bigger boys as a high school freshman, averaging 26 points, 15 rebounds and 10 assists per game with a ridiculous .700 shooting percentage. His one season of stellar play landed him on the national radar.

Born in Mobile, Alabama, Cousins flourished on the hardwood, dazzling scouts with the hands of a guard and the size of a forward. But despite a gregarious, engaging personality outside of the gym, Cousins was plagued by a reputation as a hothead on the court, a stigma he carried into college.

Cousins spent just one year at Kentucky before jumping to the Association. A fan favorite there despite playing just over 20 minutes per game, he still managed 15 points and 10 rebounds per contest. His coach, John Calipari, said Cousins was "one of the most talented big men I've ever had." Calipari went on to cite Cousins'

ball-handling skills and his "mean streak" as positives for the prospect.

In 2010–11, his rookie year, Cousins turned heads with his skill set, and he put up respectable numbers: 14.1 points per game and 8.6 rebounds. The following year, despite turmoil with then-Kings coach Paul

Westphal, Cousins' stats improved in all facets, including steals and blocks. But he wasn't living up to his potential, and the Kings continued to be awful.

At 6-foot-11 and 270 pounds, "Boogie" is one of the best bigs in the NBA. Case in point: in the third game of the 2014–15

- Named to NBA All-Rookie First Team in 2010–11
- Has played in four All-Star Games (2015–18)
- Named to All-NBA Second Team two times (2014–15, 2015–16)
- Led the NBA in offensive rebounds (265) in 2011–12
- Led the NBA in defensive rebound percentage (30.5) in 2013–14

season, he put up 34 points and 18 rebounds against Blake Griffin and the LA Clippers. In 2015–16, Cousins had a night to remember, scoring 56 points in a double OT loss to the Charlotte Hornets. He hit 21 of 30 from the field and hauled down 12 boards in one of the top individual efforts of the season from any NBA player. It was a tantalizing display of the potential the center possesses.

Cousins' success isn't without its problems. His career has been marred by his temper and penchant for technical fouls. In 2012–13, he led the NBA with 17 Ts. In 2014–15, 2015–16 and 2016–17 he followed along the same lines. But maybe Cousins' foul trouble isn't that big a deal. People don't waste a lot of breath talking about Russell Westbrook's penchant for getting T'd up. (Westbrook finished second behind Cousins in 2016–17.) The lack of emphasis on Westbrook's foul trouble seems a double standard — and perhaps linked more to Cousins' position and reputation than anything else.

Despite having his best offensive season to date in 2016–17 — he finished seventh in scoring — Cousins was traded by Sacramento at the conclusion of the 2017 All-Star Game to the New Orleans Pelicans, a move that caught everyone off guard, including the center. He finished the year in Louisiana, averaging 27 points and 11 rebounds. He dominated the paint

in 2017–18 before an Achilles injury in January sidelined him for half the season. But just before he tore up his ankle, he tore up the Chicago Bulls, posting a 44-20-10 line — only five other players in history can claim that kind of game. Up until his injury, Cousins was notching 25.2 points per game and a career-high 12.9 rebounds.

The 2018 off-season was a different story. Rehabbing, he received no offers and signed a one-year deal with the Golden State Warriors. Cousins debuted as a Warrior in January 2019, and his impact in the middle of the court was felt immediately as he

became an additional weapon for an already stacked team. He had one of his best nights as a Warrior late in the season against the Houston Rockets. He put up 28 points, 7 assists and 8 rebounds, showing the league what he's capable of night in, night out and reminding fans of his next-level talent.

In the 2019 off-season Cousins signed another one-year deal, this time with the Los Angeles Lakers. He is barely on the precipice of his prime, so the sky's the limit for his individual success. Will the change of zip code (and a little help from LeBron James) alter the course of his career?

DEMAR DEROZAN 10

IT'S BEEN HARD to label DeMar DeRozan a superstar quite yet, difficult to mention him in the company of NBA greats. But slowly, surely, quietly and diligently, the former face of the Toronto Raptors and now starting shooting guard for the San Antonio Spurs has been putting in work, and it's finally paying off, both in career numbers and team success.

The product of Compton High School and USC, DeRozan has always surprised pundits with his smooth dribbling, sweet jumper and knack for getting to the line. But make no mistake, he's always been lethal, and as a high school freshman he averaged 26.1 points and 8.4 rebounds. The talented young man, who could dunk at 12 years old, stayed loyal to his hometown high school rather than jump ship for a more prestigious place to play.

Forgoing the final three years of his NCAA eligibility after one season at USC, the athletic guard was selected by the Toronto Raptors ninth overall in 2009. While other players have shunned playing in Canada or elected to move elsewhere to pursue better opportunities to win after their entry-level contracts were complete, DeRozan stepped up to the opportunity and made it clear that Toronto was where he wanted to be. Despite several losing seasons to begin his tenure, his years in Toronto paid dividends, and DeRozan became the leader and the go-to guy on the team.

His size on the defensive end against smaller guards is difficult to get past, and he can guard undersized forwards on the wing, a versatility hard to find in the NBA. From the line, DeRozan is equally dangerous, averaging over 82 percent from the stripe. If there's one knock against the pro, it's his three-point shooting, but there's no need to

add that to his arsenal yet — he's still slashing and driving, turning around defenders with a crossover and draining difficult turnaround Js, and all that pressure helps him make it to the line.

Over the past 10 seasons, DeRozan has been a horse, logging over 34 minutes per contest. In 2014–15, however, he faced his

CAREER HIGHLIGHTS

- Has played in four All-Star Games (2014, 2016–2018)
- Named to All-NBA Second Team in 2017–18
- Named to All-NBA Third Team in 2016–17
- Is a 10-time NBA Player of the Week
- Won an Olympic gold medal with the U.S. men's basketball team in Rio in 2016

confidence oozes from his eyes, a steely look that means business. You see it in the eyes of the NBA's best, and the shooting guard is forcing commentators to include him in that category as his career stretches on. He has made the playoffs six consecutive years, including a 2016 run into the conference finals with the Raptors.

By far, the 2016–17 season will go down as one of DeRozan's finest. He finished fifth in NBA scoring, averaging over 27 points per game, and touched the 40-point mark seven times. With Kyle Lowry injured, DeRozan single-handedly dominated opponents late in the season, including a herculean 43 against division rivals the Boston Celtics. The 2017 playoffs ended in disappointment; after scraping past the Milwaukee Bucks in the first round, the Toronto Raptors fell to LeBron James and the Cleveland Cavaliers for a second straight year.

It was rinse and repeat the following season — DeRozan's last in Toronto. He had another solid campaign, averaging 23 points and 5 assists, but after getting beaten by the Cavs for a third time in the playoffs, the Raptors shipped their franchise player to San Antonio for superstar Kawhi Leonard. The trade shocked Toronto's longest-serving player as well as Raptors fans, and he drew a warm reception when he returned as a Spur in February 2019.

The trade may have been a blessing in disguise. In 2018–19 DeRozan had his most complete season yet, with 21 points, 6 assists and 6 rebounds — the latter two stats career highs. He even notched his first career triple-double against his former team in January — 21 points, 14 rebounds and 11 assists. He's been pivotal in keeping the Spurs competitive, and they reached the playoffs once again in 2019.

The boy from Compton who once called Canada his second home has now taken his talents to Texas, where the next chapter will be written. If the first part of his story is any indication, the second half of his career will be one to watch.

first lengthy layoff after tearing an adductor muscle, which forced him out for 21 games. And although it took some time to find his form, DeRozan propped up the Raptors while the team battled injuries and inconsistent play. In March 2015 DeRozan dropped a cool 35 on the Philadelphia 76ers and then followed that up with 25 against Cleveland. He has become the guy his team wants taking shots late in the game, staring down opponents and going 1-on-1 with the shot clock winding down. A quiet

POSITION CENTER / **SHOOTS** RIGHT / **HEIGHT** 7'0" / **WEIGHT** 250 LB. / **DRAFTED** 2014, PHILADELPHIA 76ERS, 3RD OVERALL

JOEL EMBIID 21

AT 7 FEET and 250 pounds, it's hard to miss Joel Embiid. The center from Cameroon isn't just physically intimidating; he's fast become one of the most recognizable personalities in the sport — a blend of good-natured competitiveness and trash-talking that's endeared him to fans in Philly and across the league. In just a few seasons, the former Kansas one-and-done has become a premier big man in the NBA, and he has his sights set on lifting Philly out of the ashes and into perennial playoff contention.

Cameroon has a long history of basketball, and Embiid isn't the only player in the NBA from this African nation. The Toronto Raptors' Pascal Siakam and the Houston Rockets' Luc Mbah a Moute also hail from Cameroon. But Embiid is the superstar, a former third overall pick in the 2014 draft. Sidelined by foot injuries in 2014–15 and 2015–16, he didn't debut in the NBA until October 2016. The wait was worth it, and he's emerged as a power center with incredible fluidity on the block.

Embiid didn't even start playing ball until he was 15 years old, and he barely spoke any English or had any training when he arrived in the United States at 16 years of age to devote himself to prep school basketball. He told *The Players' Tribune* how he watched the same DVD over and over again for three years. On the tape was Hakeem Olajuwon. "I would study the way Hakeem moved, and I would go out and try to imitate him," Embiid describes.

He was a raw talent, but doubts plagued him early on that he wouldn't make it to the NBA. Instilled with an incomparable work ethic, he pushed forward, despite humiliating moments like getting dunked on in front of an entire gym's worth of players when he first set foot on the Kansas Jayhawks' court. Embiid seems to thrive on using his defeats to fuel his successes. At Kansas, he was named Big 12 Defensive Player of the Year as a freshman while still averaging over 11 points and 8 boards. But injuries plagued him that year as well, and he missed March Madness because of a stress fracture in his back.

Embiid has been racking up accolades ever since he got healthy. He started in the 2018 and 2019 All-Star Games, made the All-NBA second team in 2018, and has consistently hoisted his squad on his back when need be. Take for example the 2018–19 season, when he started putting up stupid good numbers. How about the 30 points and 19 boards at the beginning of the season against the Milwaukee Bucks? Or the 40-point, 21-rebound game against Indiana, or the 26 points and 6 blocks versus the New York Knicks in January? He even put up a triple-double against the Orlando Magic, recording a 19-13-10 line. Or how about the monster 40-point, 15-rebound performance in mid-March against the number one Bucks? After that game, Giannis Antetokounmpo, aka the Greek Freak, said about Embiid: "He's a tough guy. He's a great defender, strong. It was kind of hard going at him."

Embiid has been stuffing the stats all season, and more importantly he's become nearly impossible to play against. For his size, he moves off the ball well. He's solid in the post and possesses a deadly shot. He finished fifth in NBA scoring, second in rebounding, and sixth in blocks and was Philadelphia's MVP all season. Embiid, Ben Simmons and Jimmy Butler made a formidable trio, especially after the team's third-place finish in the Eastern Conference. It's

a big deal — this is a team that had just 10 wins in 2015–16 and now has had back-to-back playoff seasons.

Armed with a five-year, $148 million contract, Embiid is a cornerstone of the 76ers franchise. He's come a long way since those teenage days in Cameroon, where he barely knew a ball from a hoop. After years of hard work and perseverance, he's become a diamond in the rough, and Philly has turned their fortunes around with several bright building blocks, all in the hopes of earning the shiniest prize — a championship trophy.

CAREER HIGHLIGHTS

- Named to NBA All-Rookie First Team in 2016–17
- Named to NBA All-Defensive Second Team two times (2017–18, 2018–19)
- Has played in two All-Star Games (2018, 2019)
- Named to All-NBA Second Team two times (2017–18, 2018–19)
- Finished second in rebounds per game (13.6) in 2018–19

LOS ANGELES CLIPPERS

POSITION SHOOTING GUARD–SMALL FORWARD / **SHOOTS** RIGHT / **HEIGHT** 6'9" / **WEIGHT** 220 LB. / **DRAFTED** 2010, INDIANA PACERS, 10TH OVERALL

PAUL GEORGE  13

IT WAS ONE of the freakiest injuries anyone in basketball had ever seen. In a scrimmage to decide the U.S. roster for the 2014 FIBA World Cup, Paul George suffered a gruesome broken leg when he slammed into the backboard stanchion trying to block a James Harden shot in transition defense. The injury kept him off the court for most of the 2014–15 season, and many questioned whether the forward would ever be the same player.

Back in the lineup in 2015–16, Paul averaged 23.1 points per contest to go along with 7 boards and 4.1 assists. He provided the fuel needed by the Pacers engine to reach the playoffs. He effectively put the criticism to rest and established his status among the NBA elite — something he will continue to do as he plies his trade for the Los Angeles Clippers.

At 6-foot-9 and 220 pounds, George is tall, athletic and in possession of a shot that's nearly impossible to stop even when a smaller opponent is draped all over him. That's the problem. It doesn't matter if you match up a bigger man against George — he's too smooth. If you go small, he'll use his body to get the defender out of the way.

Drafted 10th overall in 2010, George spent two years playing college ball at Fresno State in California, near his hometown of Palmdale. He wasn't as highly touted in the state of California as DeMar DeRozan, but he was a player to watch. George averaged 16.3 points in his second

and final year of college before making the jump to the NBA. His draft class was loaded with talent — John Wall and DeMarcus Cousins went first and fifth, respectively, and Utah picked Gordon Hayward just

before George. Arguably, the Pacers picked the best small forward available.

He was a one-man difference maker in the first-round playoff matchup versus the Toronto Raptors in 2015–16, stuffing

but George didn't have the type of breakout season Indiana fans were hoping for, even though he single-handedly willed the Pacers into the 2017 playoffs.

George has received a few key accolades — he was named the league's most improved player in 2013 and won gold with the U.S. men's Olympic squad in 2016. But he's got his eyes set on a different prize — one in the form of a championship ring. In June 2017, just before the free-agent deadline, the Pacers traded George to Oklahoma City for Victor Oladipo and Domantas Sabonis. This league-rocking deal suddenly gave Russell Westbrook and the Thunder squad the ammunition to rise to the top of the dominant west.

George put up some serious numbers in 2017–18, his first season in Oklahoma. He averaged 22 points per game, 2 steals and 40 percent from behind the arc. Speaking of threes, twice that season he hit eight in one game, including Game 1 of the playoffs versus Utah, when he finished with 36 points on 13 of 20 shooting. George fit in perfectly with the Thunder, and in the 2018 off-season he decided to sign with the team long term, penning a four-year max contract.

This past season has been George's best. Versus the Miami Heat, he hit 10 three-pointers and scored 43, and he hoisted a last-second buzzer beater to finish with 45 against the Utah Jazz. George remained in the MVP conversation all season for his exceptional two-way play. He finished second in the NBA in scoring and set career highs in average points (28), assists (2.2) and rebounds (8.2).

In a move that shook up the 2019 off-season, George requested a trade from Oklahoma to pair up with 2019 NBA Finals MVP Kawhi Leonard on the Los Angeles Clippers. Now, alongside veteran title-winner Leonard anything is possible for George. What's a given is that he's finally come into his own as one of the most versatile players in the league.

DeRozan on defense with his length and providing nearly all the Pacers' offense in the seven-game-series loss. He was easily the best player in the series and proved he has the skills to keep up in a tough playoff matchup.

The next season was an interesting story. He concluded 2016 with back-to-back 30-plus-point efforts, and the product of Fresno State consistently put up big numbers in 2017. He was an All-Star once again,

BLAKE GRIFFIN 23

BLAKE GRIFFIN LIKELY needs no introduction. You've probably seen him soaring through the air, high above the rim, waiting for a lob pass before slamming the ball into the bucket below. Griffin is more than just the meat and potatoes of his franchise — he's a multidimensional power forward who's quickly become one of the most versatile and exciting players in the NBA.

At 6-foot-10 and 250 pounds, it's hard to contend with his size. Griffin's a muscular, agile forward, with speed to the hoop and Superman-like ability to play above the rim. He was born in Oklahoma City and suited up for the Sooners in college. By his sophomore season, he'd emerged as the best player in the country; he declared for the draft after notching 22.7 points per game and 14.4 rebounds in his second year at Oklahoma.

Taken number one overall by the Clippers, Griffin's presence immediately changed the franchise — although it took an extra year thanks to a preseason knee injury that kept him sidelined for all of 2009–10. By the time he finally threw on a Clips jersey, Griffin's star-like abilities were obvious. He twice topped 40 points in 2010–11, dropping 44 against New York early in the season and 47 versus Indiana later that campaign. He was a unanimous choice for Rookie of the Year, becoming the first rookie since Ralph Sampson in 1984 to sweep the award. He averaged 22.1 points, 12.1 boards and 3.8 assists. But it wasn't just that. Griffin managed two triple-doubles and amassed a miraculous 63 double-doubles for the third highest total in the league. He finished three shy of that year's leader, Dwight Howard, a staggering achievement for a rookie.

Griffin's spectacular first year had shades of another great's rookie campaign. Shaquille O'Neal, the former LA Lakers and Orlando Magic star, posted 23.9 points and 13.9 rebounds his inaugural year in the league, and he added 3.5 blocks. Despite

- Named NBA Rookie of the Year for 2010–11
- Has played in six All-Star Games (2011–2015, 2019)
- Won the NBA Slam Dunk Contest in 2011
- Named to All-NBA Second Team three times (2011–12 to 2013–14)
- Named to All-NBA Third Team two times (2014–15, 2018–19)

for the first time since 2006, ringing in a new era in Los Angeles despite a second-round loss to San Antonio. In their first full season together the following year, Paul and Griffin continued to wreak havoc. Despite a slight dip in his numbers, Griffin still led the team with averages of 18 points and 8.7 boards, while Paul dished out 9.7 dimes per game. The team finished 56-26 but fell to the Memphis Grizzlies in the first round, a disappointing exit for a strong team.

Griffin has added to his game, unleashing a step-back jumper that's nearly automatic when he's left open. It used to be that Griffin would almost always take the ball to the hoop. Now defenders need to do a little guesswork. Griffin was arguably a key component in the Clippers' reaching the postseason six straight seasons, but there always seemed to be limits to how far they could go. The 2016–17 season ended with another disappointing first-round playoff exit, one in which Griffin injured his foot and needed surgery. It was a blow for long-starved Clippers fans desperate for a title and bragging rights in a crowded California market.

Griffin signed a long contract extension in 2017, only to get traded months into the 2017–18 season to the Detroit Pistons. It was a blessing in disguise. He's now playing his best ball, as evidenced by his 50-point game against the Philadelphia 76ers early in the 2018–19 season. With a career high of 24.5 points per game this past season, he's almost irreplaceable for the surging Pistons. He upped his threes per game and shot 36 percent in 2018–19 to lead Detroit's squad to the NBA playoffs.

The Pistons still haven't won a playoff game in over a decade, but at least they got to the first round — and it was thanks to Griffin's spirited play alongside another big man, Andre Drummond, who made life in the paint painful for opposing players throughout the regular season. Arguably, Drummond's coming-out party had a lot to do with Griffin's arrival in the Motor City. Sometimes a new zip code is all you need to have success.

this, O'Neal was not a unanimous selection for best rookie like Griffin. The Clippers, however, didn't make the playoffs, finishing 32-50. The team's fortunes would change when they traded for Chris Paul later that year.

The pair immediately became the core of Lob City, a high-flying, acrobatic group that was a threat from the air every time they ran the ball up court during the lockout-shortened 2011–12 season. The Clips finished 40-26 and made the postseason

PORTLAND TRAIL BLAZERS

POSITION POINT GUARD / **SHOOTS** RIGHT / **HEIGHT** 6'3" / **WEIGHT** 195 LB. / **DRAFTED** 2012, PORTLAND TRAIL BLAZERS, 6TH OVERALL

DAMIAN LILLARD  0

DAMIAN LILLARD SHOULD need no introduction to anyone who has watched the Portland Trail Blazers play during the past seven years. The point guard from Oakland has firmly established himself as the future of the franchise and one of the rising stars in the NBA.

The most impressive thing you can call a basketball player is clutch. And that's what Lillard proved himself to be in the 2014 playoffs, ending a long drought for Portland fans who'd been waiting to see their team travel beyond the first round. Some have called his game-winning basket in Game 6

versus the Houston Rockets the greatest shot in Trail Blazers history. Lillard's heroics cemented the first playoff series win in 14 years and endeared him to a fan base starving for a championship.

Nights like that will define Lillard's career for years to come. He grew up tough and quickly — you have to on the streets of Oakland. With that toughness came an obsession — he was always at the gym as a kid, looking for a game. His older brother once described him as "fearless." But Lillard was undersized and, in his own words in 2012, "overlooked." Few scholarship offers from big schools came his way, and he opted to attend Weber State in Utah, a mid-major that's not exactly on the national radar. But with a tenacity and scoring ability that saw him post 24.5 points, 5 rebounds and 4 assists per game, he was propelled to the top of the ranks by his junior season, and he skipped senior year to head into the draft, where the Trail Blazers grabbed him with the sixth pick in 2012. It was a steal.

Slow to make a name for himself out of high school, he wasted no time as a professional, entering the NBA with a bang. Lillard put up 23 points and 11 assists in his debut and never looked back, torching the league in his rookie campaign. He finished with 19 points, 6.5 assists and 3.1 rebounds per game and was a unanimous decision for Rookie of the Year. Playing all 82 games for the second straight season in his sophomore campaign (2013–14), Lillard proved

his inaugural season was no fluke, posting nearly identical numbers and increasing his threat to score from behind the arc to nearly 40 percent. He made the All-Star Team and dropped 41 points against the Sacramento Kings. And then came the playoff run, where he scored 22.9 points per contest, assisting at a rate of 6.5 per game and adding 5.1 rebounds.

The following seasons were nearly identical for Lillard. The 6-foot-3 point guard averaged nearly 36 minutes per night and routinely put up 20-plus points. (His points average climbed higher in 2015–16 to 25 points per contest and to 27 points the following season.) In 2016–17 Lillard continued to prove he's one of the best in the league, despite not receiving an invitation to the 2017 All-Star Game. He finished sixth in scoring and in the top 10 for free-throw percentage. He punctuated the end of the season with a dazzling 59-point affair against the Utah Jazz in which he drained nine three-pointers. In February 2018 against the Sacramento Kings, he scored 50 points in 29 minutes, drained eight threes and made a perfect 10 of 10 from the stripe.

Lillard appeared on the All-Star Game roster once again in 2018 and 2019, and Portland fast became a major force in the ultra-competitive west. He averaged nearly 26 points per game in 2018–19, regularly hit for over 40 a night and led the Blazers back to the promised land.

Then there was the shot seen round the world. In the first round versus the Oklahoma City Thunder, Lillard sank a series-ending three from the logo over Paul George, sending Portland fans into pandemonium and cementing his legacy as one of the most clutch shooters of his era. The Trail Blazers soared to the Western Conference finals after a seven-game thriller versus Denver, but fell to Golden State in four games.

Lillard, if you haven't realized, is a big-time budding star. If he can keep delivering, he'll continue sending fans in Rip City into a frenzy year after year.

CAREER HIGHLIGHTS

- Named NBA Rookie of the Year for 2012–13
- Named to NBA All-Rookie First Team in 2012–13
- Has played in four All-Star Games (2014, 2015, 2018, 2019)
- Named to All-NBA First Team in 2017–18
- Named to All-NBA Second Team in 2018–19

POSITION POWER FORWARD–CENTER / **SHOOTS** RIGHT / **HEIGHT** 6'10" / **WEIGHT** 251 LB. / **DRAFTED** 2008, MEMPHIS GRIZZLIES, 5TH OVERALL

KEVIN LOVE

A PRODUCT OF Lake Oswego High School in Oregon, Kevin Love was destined for the NBA. The prodigy took the west coast state by storm upon arriving in high school as a 6-foot-8 monster of a teenager. As a sophomore, he was a man among boys and once scored 50 points and 20 rebounds in one game. He led Lake Oswego to a state championship in his junior season, and during his final year, he averaged 33.9 points per game and 17 boards.

Love's only year at UCLA was equally dominant. He accrued 17.5 points per game, 10.6 rebounds and a .565 field goal percentage while taking the Bruins to the 2008 Final Four alongside future NBA superstar Russell Westbrook. The Bruins lost to the Derrick Rose–led Memphis Tigers. It would be Love's only year at college, as he declared for the draft and was taken by the Memphis Grizzlies fifth overall. Subsequently traded to the Minnesota Timberwolves, he established himself quickly, becoming one of the scariest power forwards in the game under coach Rick Adelman.

At 6-foot-10 and 251 pounds, Love's inside strength is obvious and his rebounding prowess legendary. But it's also his deft touch from 20 feet out that makes him a threat from all points on the court. And when he gets to the line, he's shot 82 percent of his free throws thus far in his career. On November 12, 2010, history was made, and Love was the centerpiece. The power forward hauled down 31 boards to go with

31 points against the New York Knicks. It was the first 30-30 game in the NBA in 28 years — since Moses Malone hit the mark in 1982. It was the most rebounds in a

game since a guy named Charles Barkley accomplished the feat. Later that season he posted a line of 43 points and 17 boards, then smoothly followed that up with a

37-23 game. He led the NBA in rebounding in 2010–11 with 15.2 boards per game.

Despite Love's stellar play, the Timberwolves were a team in decline, and following 2013–14, when he put up arguably his best offensive season to date — 26.1 points, 12.5 boards and 4.4 assists (a career best) while shooting a respectable 45.7 percent from the field — Love made it known he wanted out.

Superstar LeBron James just happened to be making his own move, and Love became a focal point as the four-time MVP returned to Cleveland. James had played with Love in the 2012 Olympics and convinced his national squad teammate to forgo an offer to be a building block for the rebuilding Los Angeles Lakers and instead help him bring a championship to Cleveland.

His first season as a Cavalier in 2014–15, though, was a learning curve for Love — sharing the rock didn't come easily to the big man who likes to have the ball flow through him. Logically, playing with LeBron means Love's numbers were down — and

in some cases, such as points per game, way down. But he came to Ohio for one thing and one thing only — to win a ring.

A shoulder injury in the first round of the 2015 playoffs derailed Love's season, and he played no part in the Cavs' finals run that year. He did, however, play pivotal roles in Cleveland's 2016 title win as well as trips to the NBA Finals the following two seasons. He made it known he'd be a force to be reckoned with throughout the playoffs, averaging over 15 points and nearly 10 rebounds per game in those three postseasons. The Cavs lost to Golden State in 2016–17 and 2017–18, but three trips to the finals and one ring were nice stamps on the résumé of a player of Love's caliber.

Things in Cleveland changed pretty quickly when Irving left for Boston and LeBron jumped ship for Hollywood. The Cavs sank to the bottom of the conference, leaving Love to hold the fort as the franchise rebuilds. Despite injuries that limited him to 22 games in 2018–19, he led the Cavs in scoring 14 times and averaged nearly

- Named NBA Most Improved Player for 2010–11
- Named to NBA All-Rookie Second Team in 2008–09
- Has played in five All-Star Games (2011, 2012, 2014, 2017, 2018)
- Ranks third in rebounds per game (11.3) among active NBA players
- Won an Olympic gold medal with the U.S. men's basketball team in London in 2012

11 rebounds a game. Off the court, he has garnered support from players and fans alike for speaking up about his battles with anxiety and advocating awareness of mental health issues.

The 31-year-old ball hawk has plenty of prime years left to establish a legacy as a multi-title winner. He's a premier power forward and center, with a deft post game and a sweet shot. With plenty of finals experience, Love is one star you can bank on for years to come.

POSITION SHOOTING GUARD / **SHOOTS** RIGHT / **HEIGHT** 6'7" / **WEIGHT** 215 LB. / **DRAFTED** 2011, GOLDEN STATE WARRIORS, 11TH OVERALL

KLAY THOMPSON 11

THE QUIETEST ONES are often the most danger-ous — the deadly assassins who sneak up quietly to silence their enemies. Klay Thompson fits that mold perfectly. And don't think the laid-back west coaster is disinterested or nonplussed. He is a premier defender and a lights-out shooter who, in his short career, already holds some of the NBA's top shooting records. For the Golden State Warriors shooting guard, this is his prime time.

When Thompson set the NBA record for most points in one quarter with 37, we should have known it would be only

the first of many jaw-dropping moments. When he's firing a shot, defenders need to look out. It could be from deep, or from the corner or off the dribble, but it's usually nothing but net. After that 37-point third quarter in early 2015, the shooting guard dropped a cool 60 points in just 29 minutes the following season against Indiana, nearly matching Kobe Bryant's 62 points in three quarters. But even that's nothing compared with Game 6 in the 2016 Western Conference finals. Facing elimination and down in the fourth quarter in Oklahoma City, Golden State turned to Klay. He made it rain, dropping 11 three-pointers — the most ever in a playoff game — en route to 41 points and the win, which launched the Warriors back into the NBA Finals. That's what you call heat check, and it likely played a role in Kevin Durant's joining Thompson and the Golden State Warriors in 2016–17.

Thompson owes some of his success to the all-star cast around him who take the pressure off. Cover Steph Curry and you leave Klay wide open. Then there's firecracker Draymond Green waiting for the rock to drive it to the hoop. It means Thompson can lurk in the shadows, bide his time and spend a ton of energy at the other end of the court guarding the opposing team's best shooter.

The 6-foot-7, 215-pound shooting guard is the perfect blend of size and speed. Thompson's durability is something to behold — he rarely gets hurt and rarely

takes a night off defensively. If pouring his energy into his defense means he must sacrifice points, so be it. He's got a former MVP named Steph Curry in the backcourt to pick up the offensive slack.

Raised in Lake Oswego, Oregon, where he played alongside future NBAer Kevin Love, Thompson was the toast of the town at the University of Washington, playing three seasons and averaging 21.6 points his final year. After being drafted 11th overall by Golden State, Thompson took his talents to California, where he's been happy to play second fiddle for a perennial championship team. That doesn't mean he doesn't want to get his due when he's feeling it, as we've seen again and again with Thompson. There may be no player in the league who can score in waves like he can.

Like Curry's father, Dell, Thompson's father, Mychal, was a pro basketball player in the 1980s, the first overall pick in the 1978 draft who suited up with the Portland Trail Blazers, the San Antonio Spurs and the LA Lakers, winning two titles late in his career. He's now a radio broadcaster for the Lakers. "He's my biggest believer," Thompson said about his father in 2014. "He always told me . . . that I could make it to the NBA if I just stayed humble and worked hard."

That hard work led him to his third championship in 2018, but he might be remembered most for sparking a 17-point comeback in Game 6 of the Western Conference finals against the Houston Rockets, hoisting up three after three to finish with 35 points. Putting back-to-back titles on his résumé bolsters the fact he's an essential part of the Golden State dynasty, and he'll go down as one of the greatest shooters of his era. Thompson also shows little sign of slowing down: in October 2018, he set the record for most made threes in a game (14), finishing with 52 points in just 27 minutes on the floor. And when Durant suffered a calf injury versus Houston in the second round of the 2019 playoffs, Thompson stepped up, dropping back-to-back 27-point games before Golden State

CAREER HIGHLIGHTS

swept Portland on the way to a fifth straight NBA Finals.

While Thompson will sit most of 2019–20 with a torn ACL suffered in Game 6 of the NBA Finals, the quiet superstar still has three NBA championship rings, an Olympic gold medal and several entries in the NBA record book because of his shooting performances. His father always wanted him to be a Laker, but with the way things are going, Thompson may be a Warrior for life.

- Named to NBA All-Rookie First Team in 2011–12
- Has played in five All-Star Games (2015–2019)
- Won the NBA Three-Point Contest in 2016
- Named to All-NBA Third Team two times (2014–15, 2015–16)
- Won an Olympic gold medal with the U.S. men's basketball team in Rio in 2016

POSITION POINT GUARD / **SHOOTS** RIGHT / **HEIGHT** 6'4" / **WEIGHT** 210 LB. / **DRAFTED** 2010, WASHINGTON WIZARDS, 1ST OVERALL

JOHN WALL 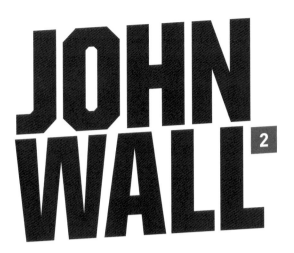 2

JOHN WALL IS as pure a point guard as they come: lightning-quick first step, excellent shot, deadly passer. The latter was especially true in the 2014–15 season when he started averaging 10 assists per game en route to a starting All-Star appearance (his second at the time). With Wall's leadership, the Washington Wizards are perennial playoff contenders. A teammate like Bradley Beal doesn't hurt either, but it's Wall's magic that stokes the engine of the team, and he's finally getting his due.

The 6-foot-4 guard didn't have a typical childhood — his father was incarcerated just after John was born and passed away when he was just 9. Wall was a tempestuous kid on and off the court in his hometown of Raleigh, North Carolina. Anger issues made several coaches ban him from high-level basketball camps when he was a teenager. But he finally got his act together, and by the time he graduated, he led his team to the state championship, averaging 19.7 points, 9 assists and just over 8 rebounds.

He was a one-and-done at the University of Kentucky, putting up 16.6 points and 6.5 dimes per contest before he was selected first overall by the Wizards in the 2010 draft. He recorded a triple-double six games into his rookie season (19 points, 13 assists and 10 rebounds), but the Wizards were simply horrible, losing 59 games. They lost 46 in the lockout-shortened 2011–12 season and 59 again the following year. Some players may have gotten used to all the losing. Not Wall. It might be hard to imagine such a once-selfish person on the basketball court becoming one of the league's most unselfish players. But that is exactly what Wall did — and how he led the Wizards out of the NBA hinterlands.

He's averaging more than 9 assists per game during his career and has emerged as a basketball player masquerading as an artist: he drives down the lane and spins 360 for layups; throws behind-the-back passes to teammates; startles opponents with a "yo-yo" dribble and a fake pass that creates space for him and his teammates.

- Named to NBA All-Rookie First Team in 2010–11
- Named to NBA All-Defensive Second Team in 2014–15
- Has played in five All-Star Games (2014–2018)
- Named to All-NBA Third Team in 2016–17
- Ranks second in assists per game (9.22) among active NBA players

former Kentucky product hoisting this team on his back, especially in the first round of the 2015 playoffs, when he torched the Toronto Raptors during a four-game sweep. But a wrist fracture at the beginning of the second round forced him to the bench, and despite a valiant return later in the series, the Wizards were bounced by the Atlanta Hawks. The team failed to make the postseason the following year, but Wall continued his ascension into the upper stratosphere of the NBA. Named Eastern Conference Player of the Month in December 2015, he followed up that honor with four triple-doubles in the second half of the season despite carrying bumps and bruises along the way.

In 2016–17, after surgery on both knees, Wall saw his points per game climb three points while still maintaining the second highest assist rate in the NBA. Washington defeated the Atlanta Hawks in the first round of the playoffs, with Wall's 42 points, 8 assists and 4 steals in Game 6 the final nail in the coffin. His performance in the second round was just as epic: in Game 6 against the Boston Celtics, with Washington facing elimination, Wall hit a game-winning three-pointer that sent the home crowd into a frenzy and forced a Game 7 in Boston, which they lost.

The 2017–18 season started with hope, but a knee injury sidelined Wall for half the year. The Wiz still made the playoffs but fell at the hands of the Toronto Raptors despite the point guard's 28 points and 14 dimes in Game 3 of the first round. The next season started off much the same, with Beal and Wall doing their thing and hope of playoff contention blossoming in the U.S. capital once again. But another season-ending injury derailed Wall, who, much to the disappointment of Wizards fans, is expected to sit until February 2020.

When he's healthy, the man with quick hands and faster feet is one of the best guards in the game today. The question remains: will he bring Washington its first championship in over 40 years?

He began the 2014–15 season with two 30-point affairs in the first five games. In December he recorded 17 assists twice and started that month with seven straight games of 10-plus assists, putting up only one game of fewer than 8 helpers. By the All-Star break, he was leading the team in points, assists and steals, the same as he did in 2013–14. It's hard to imagine where the Wizards would be without the

THE DUNK CONTEST

ON FEBRUARY 9, 1991, it's fair to say few inside the Charlotte Coliseum had heard of a 6-foot shooting guard named Dee Brown. In the past, winners of the NBA Slam Dunk Contest — stars such as Dominique Wilkins, Michael Jordan and Spud Webb, who would define their early careers with the exposure at the annual All-Star Game — were already known to the masses. Not so for the Celtics rookie. When the unknown shooting guard leaned down, pumped up his Reebok shoes and leapt toward the basket with one arm draped over his eyes, he entered NBA lore, winning the 1991 dunk contest with the now-famous no-look dunk. Immediately immortalized thereafter on posters and in magazines, the jam heard 'round the world prompted Magic Johnson to say on air that February night: "Everybody at home, don't try that. That is unbelievable." The dunk is so iconic that Brown's daughter, now a WNBA player, cannot escape questions

Zach LaVine, the 2015 dunk champ, slams under the spotlight during the 2015 competition.

about her father's moment in the spotlight nearly 30 years ago.

More so than Jordan's stretch slam from the foul line, Wilkins' windmill or Vince Carter's between the legs, Brown's no-looker sent the dunk contest to another stratosphere and etched his name on the lips of young fans for years down the road. A vital change had occurred: no longer was the evening designed for a select group of well-known individuals. No longer was it a superstar's athleticism shining through. Dee Brown was just a kid, an everyman, wearing second-tier shoes and flashing a Gumby flattop haircut. His creative, organic flair began an era at the All-Star Game that encouraged out-of-box thinking, something that would become a trademark for the next generation of NBA players for years to come.

IN THE (NEAR) BEGINNING

The name Larry Nance likely conjures up a whole lot of . . . diddly squat. But in 1984, Nance was named the winner of the first NBA Slam Dunk Contest, edging out the legendary Julius Erving for the $10,000 prize. The contestants that year in Denver were a ragtag group — legends like Erving, unheralded middle-of-the-road 80s NBA stars like Darrell Griffith and Michael Cooper, and a few off-the-map rookies. It was a motley crew to say the least.

As for marquee stars, Dr. J was already a household name inside and outside the league, nearing the end of his career. He gained early fame for his history-altering dunk from the free-throw line in 1976 at the ABA All-Star Game, the first dunk contest of its kind, also held in Denver, and he was widely known around the NBA for spectacular in-game slams. Atlanta Hawks stud Dominique Wilkins — drafted third overall in the 1982 draft — was still young but already making a name for himself as a power-slamming specialist known as "the Human Highlight Film." Trail Blazers guard Clyde "the Glide" Drexler may have been a first-year player and unknown outside the Portland area, but anyone who followed his career in college knew he was a product of "Phi Slama Jama," the Houston squad that defined their team around lob plays and high-flying

dunks. (To all those Clippers fans, that's the original Lob City.) Then there was all 7-foot-4 of Ralph Sampson, the former Rookie of the Year and the tallest player in the competition. The judges were equally offbeat and included a Colorado congresswoman and a New York Mets catcher.

Dr. J was the man to beat of course, and in 2014, Darrell Griffith (whose nickname was Dr. Dunkenstein) said: "[Erving] still had hops. He had them bear claw hands. He could grab the ball like it was an orange." Fan participation included scribbling numbers on handmade cards to rate dunks, something that gained in popularity as time went on, becoming a staple in the stands and at the judges table as the contest progressed. And although Nance may have been proclaimed the winner by points — and bought a Camaro with his winnings — the moment of the night belonged to Erving when he

Dr. J is in full flight at the first-ever professional slam dunk competition, which took place at the 1976 ABA All-Star Game. Dr. J won the competition with this jam that started from the free-throw line.

revisited his '76 ABA slam by running the length of the floor, leaping from behind the charity stripe once again and scoring the first perfect score of the night. The crowd went wild. "The whole show was just a buildup for Dr. J," contestant Michael Cooper said years later. "You could feel the electricity in the gym."

Jordan would re-create Dr. J's dunk several years later in 1988 — it too immortalized poster form, perhaps even one that Dee Brown had in his room. Posters were currency in the pre-Internet NBA, street cred for the athletically inclined teenager, a way to show off one's allegiance to a team or a newfound hero who could do amazing things with a basketball. Those posters of high-flying heroes showing off their moves in the dunk contest populated the bedrooms of basketball fans years before kids traded in still images for YouTube videos.

Although the modern-day dunk competition may have morphed into more spectacle than contest — with cool sneakers and trick dunks the norm — there's something still exciting about seeing one

man on the court, seconds before he leaps in the air, trying something no one has ever dared attempt. It is the moment where "what if?" becomes reality.

THE LAST GREAT DUNK

The 1990s following Dee Brown's signature slam was a largely forgettable era of dunking, and by the time Brent Barry — aka the only white guy to ever win the Slam Dunk Contest — was declared the winner in 1996, times had truly changed. The NBA shelved the contest for several years in a bid to regroup, and then along came Vince Carter.

The North Carolina product was a second-year player for the Toronto Raptors in 2000, the year the dunk contest ticked upward once again. That season, the fifth overall pick from the 1998 draft averaged a career-high 25.7 points per game, leading the young Raps into the playoffs for the first time in franchise history. Carter was a throwback to the old dunkers — a fluid mix of creativity, raw power and ingenuity that immediately launched him into the mix of the greatest to ever slam. His between-the-legs midair jam to claim the title vaulted him to the top of the dunking charts. Up until 2014–15, when youngster Zach LaVine wowed the crowd, many casual fans, and LaVine himself, would say Carter was the last great dunker thanks to a plethora of moves that included a 360 windmill, an elbow in the rim and the aforementioned between-the-legs dunk. What's undeniable is that night in DC has been etched in NBA lore and is still dubbed "the last great dunk contest."

With the passage of time and Carter now a 42-year-old veteran bouncing from contract to contract, many have looked back on what that dunk symbolized for the entire country of Canada. He was quickly named "Air Canada," and "Vinsanity" arrived full force north of the border. It was a marketer's dream, much the same as when Reebok captured the zeitgeist of Dee Brown. The Raptors were desperately seeking legitimacy after a series of losing seasons to begin their tenure. Carter provided that, and if not for a game-ending clanker in the seventh contest of the Raptors' 2001 second-round playoff series versus the Allen Iverson–led Philadelphia 76ers, Toronto may have done some damage in the Eastern Conference that year.

What no one could have predicted was that a young generation of Canadian basketball fans would gravitate to Carter like moths to a flame. Soon they would be attempting Carter's awe-inspiring slams when they got older. In late 2014, Carter was honored during the first quarter of a Grizzlies–Raptors game. He looked back on his time in Toronto and the impact it had on the fans. "All of a sudden, after that first playoff win . . . everybody wanted to pick up a basketball. It was fantastic," he said. Among those fans: a seven-year-old Nik Stauskas, a Mississauga native and now a Cleveland Cavalier, and a five-year-old Andrew Wiggins, 2014–15 Rookie of the Year. Carter's own hero was Dr. J, and although the doctor may have inspired a legion of dunk enthusiasts, he didn't impact an entire nation like Carter.

IN THE BEGINNING

The origins of dunking date back to the early part of the 20th century. A *New York Times* writer described Joe Fortenberry, the captain of the 1936 U.S. men's basketball team, as "pitch[ing] the ball downward into the hoop, much like a cafeteria customer dunking a roll in coffee." Although this may have popularized the term nationally, dunk was in fact used to describe the play of stuffing the ball in the hoop in several other smaller newspapers prior to the *Times* during the early part of the 1930s. (Los Angeles Lakers play-by-play announcer Chick Hearn, who voiced the team for 42 years before his death in 2002, is widely acknowledged as creating the saying "slam dunk" with specificity to Wilt Chamberlain.) For years following, many in the game, from general managers to coaches, tried to eliminate dunking, or at the very least, raise the rim

Michael Jordan pays homage to Dr. J and his legendary 1976 charity-stripe slam with his own dunk from the stripe at the 1988 Slam Dunk Contest.

to 12 feet to thwart the practice. An underlying subtext, especially by the 1950s and 1960s, was more than likely the increasing number of African-American players in the game and their ability to dunk more often than their white counterparts. Beyond any racial sub-text, the prevailing opinion was that as players were getting taller, dunking was changing the game, and in 1940, one American wrote: "Many people claim that there is no premium on accuracy. That instead of beautiful shooting, slap happy basketball has resulted with wild throwing from every possible angle calculated to get the ball into range of the backboards where the skyscraper boys bat it down for two points."

The three-point line that emerged in the NBA in 1979, basketball's version of a home run, was a direct response to a league that had changed, especially with the likes of massive centers skilled in the art of slamming, including Kareem Abdul-Jabbar, Bill Russell and Chamberlain. The NCAA even banned dunking for nearly a decade following Abdul-Jabbar's dominance at UCLA in the 60s, when he won three straight national championships, compiling a record of 88-2. Adding a three-point line — thanks to pressure and ingenuity from ABA commish George Mikan in 1967 — lengthened the game, creating a faster, more up-tempo pace that took the focus away from the paint and allowed guards to flourish. What we see today is a guard-heavy game that's focused on hitting an open man for three in transition, or moving the ball around the perimeter to find an open shot, rather than feeding a big man like Abdul-Jabbar in the paint.

MODERN-DAY DUNKS

But it's not raining threes for everyone. Just ask Zach LaVine. In 2015, a much-needed uplift occurred in the dunking department thanks to the jaw-dropping performance of the 19-year-old shooting guard. In an age where posters are obsolete and six-second Internet videos and flashing GIFs appear mere moments after a live play, the rising star did not disappoint. He confidently donned a No. 23 Michael Jordan jersey and mimicked a *Space Jam* dunk, going through the legs and up for a reverse one-hander. It was sick. He flipped the ball in the air again on the second attempt and then went around his own back in midair, perhaps the most innovative of his four dunks. LaVine had the select group of NBA All-Stars flying out of their seats in amazement. For a contest that desperately needed a shot in the arm after several lackluster years — Dr. J had said the year prior, "You might never get back to the day when you've got the two best players in the league . . . facing off, like you did in the heyday" — LaVine delivered, at least in terms of a solo effort. Was it on par with Carter, Erving, Wilkins and MJ? Quite possibly. LaVine has called Carter "the best dunker of all time." But now, at the very least, the kid deserves to be mentioned with the greats, particularly since the contest itself has suffered some growing pains throughout the last decade and because he repeated as champion the following year in an unforgettable back-and-forth duel with Orlando's Aaron Gordon. In fact, LaVine's battle with Gordon is being hailed as one of the best contests in years, with LaVine just escaping defeat thanks to a flying one-hander from just before the free-throw line. Gordon, for his part, had the dunk of the night, leaping over a mascot and going under the legs for a left-handed jam.

So what is it exactly about LaVine's (or, for that matter, Gordon's) performances that stand out? That "wow" factor. All great dunkers have it. A sense of showmanship, talent and raw power all wrapped into one. Sure, Dwight Howard's Superman cape in 2008 was fun, but was it awe-inspiring? Hardly. Steve Nash's soccer header to Amar'e Stoudemire was crafty and clever, but come on. Gerald Green blowing out a candle in 2007 on a cupcake was kind of hard? Was it really that cool when 5-foot-9 Nate Robinson launched himself

Two-time dunk champion Dominique Wilkins, known for his aggressive rim-shaking slams, pounds this ball down at the 1988 Slam Dunk Contest.

over former winner Spud Webb? Sure, for a half-second and for the sheer fact he could elevate that high. Robinson — a three-time dunk contest champ, who also jumped over the aforementioned Howard — undoubtedly wowed the crowd. But something beyond simple elevation is needed to capture the imagination of the fans and become legendary. (Arguably, Webb's two-handed reverse in 1986, after lobbing the ball in the air 10-plus feet, was purer in form and 20 years earlier. Plus, he was only 5-foot-7, and watching Webb spring from an average man's height to the rim is pure theater.)

Like Webb's gravity-defying leap, the greatest dunks in the history of the contest have always been simple in concept, difficult in execution, pure in power. Take Wilkins, "the Human Highlight Film," two-time winner of the dunk contest, one in 1985, another in 1990. In '85, up against his longtime dunking rival, Jordan, Wilkins' windmill dunk helped secure his status as an elite player and put the Hawks on the map. Forever in the shadow of the Bulls star — he consistently

Zach LaVine pays homage to both Michael Jordan and Vince Carter with his Toon Squad through-the-legs slam that helped him win the 2015 title.

finished second in league scoring to MJ — that was one night where Wilkins came out on top. In 2015, Wilkins described his own style as bringing an element of "flare and power to the dunk contest." The Hawks star certainly did that in '85.

Although Jordan would go on to defeat Wilkins famously in 1988 by launching himself from (almost) the charity stripe à la Dr. J, because the All-Star weekend occurred in Chicago, many, including Wilkins, believed MJ's perfect score for his final dunk was blatant home favoritism. Wilkins, in 2014, even acknowledged in an interview that the famously competitive Jordan once told him: "You probably won. You know it, I know it. But we're in Chicago. What can I tell you?" Wilkins went on to say that of the five dunk contests he participated in, he "won four, but got credit for two." All said, it was a natural rivalry from two great competitors of the game, and something rarely seen in the modern era, particularly as many competitors now are rookies or up-and-coming stars in the league without much history. Who knows — maybe the Gordon–LaVine rivalry is just beginning.

SO WHERE DO we go from here? LaVine may have changed the game going forward, incorporating old-style dunks with a modern twist and making us all forget about the recent exploits of Robinson and Howard. In a clip that aired before the 2015 contest, a young LaVine discussed his early obsession with watching old dunk contests, particularly Jordan, something Carter admitted to doing as well. It showed, and maybe that's the way to a new era — look to the past. Kids need to be inspired by individuals, not spoon-fed by the league, and the NBA has done an excellent job of identifying superstars, or dunking artists like LaVine, and marketing them to fans. (Perhaps that's why NBA superstars have 10 times more Twitter followers than baseball players.)

Moving forward, the contest will likely oscillate between the gimmicky approach and a pure, no-holds-barred one that feels more like something that would happen organically on the playground. (Your honor, we present exhibit number one in the gimmicky category from the 2017 dunk contest: DeAndre Jordan grabbing the ball from DJ Khaled and leaping over an entire DJ booth.) While Dr. J's 1976 free-throw dunk looks relatively pedestrian to modern-day jammers, watching him palm the ball, back up and run the length of the court, and leap from the line was a sight to behold back then; it was pure spectacle, akin to something Evel Knievel might have pulled off. The thrill of the improbable is where the dunk contest should reside. When Dee Brown pumped up his Reeboks, he set the stage, and from there he simply leaned down, took off and covered his eyes while the world held its breath.

INTERNATIONAL STARS

LUKA DONCIC

GORAN DRAGIC

DALLAS MAVERICKS

POSITION SHOOTING GUARD / **SHOOTS** RIGHT / **HEIGHT** 6'7" / **WEIGHT** 218 LB. / **DRAFTED** 2018, ATLANTA HAWKS, 3RD OVERALL

LUKA DONCIC 77

LIKE A MAGICIAN, Luka Doncic isn't going to explain his bag of tricks anytime soon. Good thing the jaw-dropping start to his career doesn't need explaining because it's right there in your face, day in, day out. Circus-shot threes. Behind-the-back dribbles. Step-back after step-back behind the arc. When the rookie wasn't crossing up defensive players, he was driving to the basket or dishing it off, pick and roll style, to his bigs. In just his first year of the NBA, Luka "Magic" took the league by storm, but wait — he's still got a few tricks up his sleeve.

Growing up in the small European country of Slovenia (with a population of two million, roughly the same as metropolitan Houston), the 20-year-old's road to the NBA has been far from traditional. He jetted off to the EuroLeague at just 16 years of age, signing with powerhouse club Real Madrid Baloncesto, one of the best pro basketball teams outside of the NBA. Two years later, he led the team to a championship and was named MVP — something unheard of for a player so young. Even then, he was still relatively unknown before draft day in 2018, but whispers started making their way across the Atlantic before the draft about a possible superstar waiting to make his entrance from stage right.

Doncic's father, Sasa, played for Union Olimpija (now known as KK Petrol Olimpija), the 2007–08 Slovenian league champions. Goran Dragic, now a point guard for the Miami Heat and the only other Slovenian in the NBA, was a young prospect then, and in 2017 he gave an interview about the young kid who watched every game that season.

"[Doncic] would always sit under the basket," Dragic told ESPN. "Every time at halftime when we came out from the locker room he would always be shooting the ball. I always have this memory." The little gym rat who watched his father's team play would excel as a young teenager in the capital city of Ljubljana, rarely playing with kids his own age and excelling quickly.

(considered the greatest shooter to ever come out of Europe) started trickling out of the mouths of scouts eager to cash in on the magic. At just 17 years old, Doncic lifted Slovenia to the EuroBasket Championship in 2017, torching teams loaded with the Gasol brothers and Mavericks teammate Kristaps Porzingis. He had arrived, and he was ready for what lay ahead.

Drafted third overall by the Atlanta Hawks, Doncic was traded on draft day to Dallas for the rights to point guard Trae Young. The trade was the talk of the NBA, and while Young could pan out to be a mini Steph Curry, Doncic is already the full package. Listed at 6-foot-7 and 218 pounds, he straddles the role of small forward and guard. His ball skills are point guard-esque, and his knockdown shooting is already the stuff of legends. Take his corner three versus the Portland Trail Blazers in December 2018, with no time on the clock, to send the game into overtime. Falling back into the Portland bench, Doncic launched a hope and a prayer high into the sky, and it fell through the net. Among many NBA highlights from 2018–19, it ranks right up there, along with his half-court bank shot at the halftime buzzer versus the Celtics in early January, a deep three against Houston in November and a half-court buzzer beater late in the season against Brooklyn.

The Dallas Mavericks are a team in transition. As Dirk Nowitzki's squad for two decades, the team is passing the torch to another Euro star, and for the fan base, it's certainly taking the sting out of seeing the legendary German's career come to an end. But it's safe to say Mavs fans aren't looking back at past glories but are ready for the future. The Rookie of the Year finished with 21.2 points, 7.8 rebounds and 6 assists, heady stats for a first-year pro.

Is Doncic the next Steve Nash, the two-time MVP who rose out of obscurity to take the NBA by storm? Is he the heir apparent to Petrovic, lionized for his work ethic and talent? Or is he something different, someone totally unique that we've never seen before? Bet on the latter.

CAREER HIGHLIGHTS

- Named NBA Rookie of the Year for 2018–19
- Named to NBA All-Rookie First Team in 2018–19
- Named Rookie of the Month five times in 2018–19
- Ranked third all-time for most triple-doubles in a rookie season
- Named EuroLeague MVP in 2018, the youngest winner in league history

His then-coach Lojze Sisko remembered him as a "magnetic personality," one who possessed a deadly combination: ruthless competitiveness and an off-the-charts basketball IQ. At 13, he scored 54 points, 11 rebounds and 10 assists for Olimpija in the title game of the Lido di Roma tournament. Comparisons to the Minnesota Timberwolves' Spanish guard Ricky Rubio and the late great Croatian Drazen Petrovic

POSITION POINT GUARD–SHOOTING GUARD / **SHOOTS** LEFT / **HEIGHT** 6'3" / **WEIGHT** 190 LB. / **DRAFTED** 2008, SAN ANTONIO SPURS, 45TH OVERALL

GORAN DRAGIC 7

EUROPE HAS BECOME a hotbed for NBA talent over the past decade or so, and perhaps no player better exemplifies that basketball truly is an international sport than Goran Dragic, who hails from the tiny country of Slovenia. He's emerged as one of the best guards in the game, and after several successful seasons in Phoenix, he's now the starting point guard for the Miami Heat.

After an injury derailed his budding career on the soccer field, Dragic turned to the hardcourt. He was immediately hooked, waking up at 3:00 a.m. to watch NBA stars such as Michael Jordan and Allen Iverson. In 2012 he said, "Inside my blood, I love basketball." He tore up the Slovenian league as a youngster and helped lead the U-20 team to a gold medal at the 2004 FIBA championship. Dragic was drafted 45th overall in 2008 by the San Antonio Spurs but was quickly swapped to the Suns. He started slowly, coming off the bench his first three seasons in Phoenix. "I was not aggressive enough," he said, looking back at his early years. His coach told him to forget about the mistakes, but it took a while to sink in. He had an especially difficult time dealing with the larger NBA shot-blockers.

Midway through his third season, the Slovenian was moved to Houston, where he earned backup minutes while continuing to put up respectable numbers. The following season, Dragic finally started, and in 66 games that year posted what at that point was his best line — 11.7 points per game, 5.3 assists and a career high 80.5 percent from the stripe.

As a free agent, the point guard returned to Phoenix, where he was given the chance to start — flourishing as one of the top players in the game at his position. His numbers in 2013–14 were a career best; 20.3 points per game, 5.9 assists and a smooth .505 field goal percentage helped Dragic emerge as one of the purest shooters in the NBA. He was deadly from behind the arc, converting chances at more than 40 percent — and his

defense was good too, with 1.4 steals per contest.

Dragic's go-to move is a nearly unstoppable step-back jumper that is difficult to guard effectively. He sets up the shot by dribbling hard right before launching backward off his left foot to give him separation from his defender and a clean look at the bucket. The shot is very similar to that of fellow international star Dirk Nowitzki, who's used it to climb into the NBA's top-10 all-time scorers. It helps that Dragic is a natural lefty, another difference maker that makes him difficult to defend.

Nearing the trade deadline in 2015, the Suns had a logjam at point guard and ended up dealing Dragic and his younger brother, Zoran, to Miami for picks and veteran role players. In his 26-game sample with Miami, he continued to play well, improving to 80 percent from the stripe and 5.3 assists per game. In the off-season he signed a five-year, $90 million deal to stay in Florida.

Dragic's shifty moves and pure jumping ability are two assets that add several different looks to the Heat offense. He's a pure point guard and a key piece the team has been missing since the LeBron James/ Dwyane Wade/Chris Bosh years. Pairing Dragic with center Hassan Whiteside, the Heat made it to the second round of the 2016 playoffs and then overcame an awful 11-30 start to the 2016–17 season to nearly steal the eighth seed, which opened the NBA's eyes to a young crop of hopefuls and a group of savvy vets led by Dragic. The Slovenian ended the year with 20.3 points, 5.8 assists and 40.5 percent three-point shooting in 73 games.

In 2018–19, Dragic averaged 13.7 points per game and 4.8 assists in just 36 games as he battled through injuries. With veteran Dwyane Wade's retirement, the young Heat squad has become Dragic's team. Going forward he'll mentor not only his young teammates but also his fellow countryman Luka Doncic, whose rookie year in Dallas

took the NBA by storm. The two played against each other in an NBA matchup for the first time in March 2019. Nearly 2,000 Slovenians turned out for the unique affair, one in which Dragic had his best game of the season, notching a triple-double with 23 points, 12 assists and 11 rebounds.

For the point guard from across the world, just making it to the NBA is a success story. Competing at the highest level and inspiring a new generation of players are whole different ball games.

CAREER HIGHLIGHTS

- Named NBA Most Improved Player for 2013–14
- Played in the 2018 NBA All-Star Game
- Named to All-NBA Third Team in 2013–14
- Is a member of the NBA's 20-50-40 club (points, FG %, 3PT %)
- Is a two-time Stankovic Cup champion with Slovenia (2007, 2010)

MARC GASOL  33

MARC GASOL WAS always good — but he was also the younger brother of star NBA player Pau, he of two championship rings with the Los Angeles Lakers. It's taken several years to establish himself among the NBA's elite, but the younger Gasol is finally making his own mark. The Memphis Grizzlies, where he plied his trade for most of his career, were once a perennial playoff team in the Western Conference thanks to one of the most dominant centers in the game. Now, he's taken his talents north to Toronto, where he helped bring a championship to Raptors fans.

Gasol's early life was spent in Spain, but by the time Pau had been drafted by Memphis, the Gasols had moved to Germantown, Tennessee. Marc played his final two years of high school ball in the Memphis area before returning to his home country to further his craft in the Liga ACB. That time in Spain paid off in spades — Marc was named Spanish League MVP in 2008 — and the Lakers drafted the center late in the second round in 2007. His rights were traded later that year — for his brother Pau, in fact — and Marc became a cornerstone of the Grizzlies. At times, they challenged for best NBA team. With the core three of Gasol, Zach Randolph and Mike Conley, the Grizz threw opponents around the league into fits, playing old-school, slow-tempo, defense-first basketball that bucked the current trend toward three-point shooting and a transition game.

Much of that success fell on the shoulders of the 7-foot-1 Gasol, whose emergence as one of the most consistent centers in the game hasn't gone unnoticed.

Marc's always had some serious shoes to fill — his brother was Rookie of the Year and alongside Kobe Bryant dominated the league, winning two championships. And

Marc's weight was always an issue. Not so in 2014–15 — his former teammate Mike Conley, upon seeing Gasol compete in the 2014 FIBA championship, barely recognized his center. "It look[ed] like he lost 50 pounds," Conley remarked early in the season about the 2012–13 Defensive Player of the Year. That season, he hauled down

7.8 rebounds and had 1.7 blocks playing center for the league's best defensive team, while setting career highs in free-throw percentage at .848 and leading all centers in assists with 318.

What he needed to add to his game was offense. The weight loss entering the 2014–15 season immediately made him a scoring threat, and the combo of deft touch from the 20-foot range, a reliable three-point shot and a body big enough to bang inside is lethal. It's also allowed him to hang longer in tough physical games.

But it's the intangibles he provides on the court that truly helped Memphis excel and why Toronto traded for the big. Whether he's dropping turnaround jumpers or boxing out other big men on the defensive end, Gasol's game has flourished in all facets. In 2015 the Grizz admirably lost in the second round to the eventual champion Golden State Warriors, but it wasn't due to lack of effort on Gasol's part — he averaged 20 and 10 over 11 playoff games. Despite an injury that sidelined him for the second half of the 2015–16 season, Gasol registered his first career triple-double versus the Houston Rockets, the first Grizzlies player to accomplish the feat since Pau in 2007.

Trimmer and faster than ever before, Gasol is undeniably one of the best two-way centers in the game today. In 2016–17, he averaged career highs in points (19.5) and assists (4.6) while adding a deadly three-pointer to his arsenal. He split his 11th season in 2018–19 between Memphis and Toronto and was a veteran presence on the Raptors following the February trade. In 26 regular-season games, he slowly grew into the veteran pass-first center the team craved. His season stats — 13.6 points, 7.9 rebounds, 4.4 assists — may be down a touch from his career averages, but it's the other elements Gasol brings that make him a valuable addition to any team. The trade paid off in spades in the playoffs as the Raps dominated the postseason.

Gasol started at center during the Raptors' magical playoff run, delivering key

defensive moments against opposing bigs and chipping in with top-of-the-arc threes that propelled the Raptors to victory. Marc now joins Pau among NBA champions, making them the first sibling duo to earn the coveted rings.

With Pau close to retirement, Marc has supplanted his brother as one of the most effective international centers in the NBA and now ranks among the league's best, period.

CAREER HIGHLIGHTS

- Named NBA Defensive Player of the Year for 2012–13
- Has played in three All-Star Games (2012, 2015, 2017)
- Named to All-NBA First Team in 2014–15
- Ranks eighth in the NBA in blocks (1,158) among active players
- Won an Olympic silver medal with the Spanish men's basketball team in Beijing in 2008 and London in 2012

POSITION CENTER / **SHOOTS** RIGHT / **HEIGHT** 7'1" / **WEIGHT** 245 LB. / **DRAFTED** 2013, DENVER NUGGETS, 27TH OVERALL

RUDY GOBERT 27

THERE ARE TWO sides to Rudy Gobert. One moment he's a tenacious, take-no-prisoners big man plying his trade for the Utah Jazz, noted for his physical presence in the paint; the next he's a softy who teared up recalling his mom's anguish when he was snubbed for the 2019 All-Star Game. He embodies strength and physical toughness paired with a passion for the game — a winning combination that shone through during Gobert's breakout season and that means he'll be one to watch going forward.

At 7-foot-1 and 245 pounds, the native of France was selected late in the first round of the 2013 draft, 27th overall, by the Denver Nuggets. He was traded that night to Utah — aka Swat Lake City — and soon became the focal point of a team desperate for change. What fans got was a European who is tough as nails. Gobert's untraditional route from the French league to the NBA is a testament to his talent and his will, and he follows in the footsteps of Charlotte Hornets veteran Tony Parker as one of the best Frenchmen to play at this level. Gobert hails from Saint-Quentin, a town northeast of Paris. He grew up with his mother and was a kid with boundless energy who played any sport he could. His father was a former pro basketball player, and like father, like son, Gobert took to hoops. He was so talented that soon the center moved on his own to a different city so he could play ball for a good junior team. It paid off, paving his path to the NBA.

- Named NBA Defensive Player of the Year two times (2017–18, 2018–19)
- Named to NBA All-Defensive First Team three times (2016–17 to 2018–19)
- Named to All-NBA Second Team in 2016–17
- Led the NBA in blocks (214) in 2016–17
- Led the NBA in field goal percentage (.669) in 2018–19

Gobert's rookie season was one to forget for Utah Jazz fans — the team won only 25 games, and the Frenchman didn't play that many minutes — but Gobert certainly won't forget it. Nor will he forget posting up against Jazz great Karl Malone, who offered to run Gobert through some drills during his rookie year. After guarding Malone, Gobert described him as "the strongest man I've ever seen in my life," and Malone's strength even in retirement inspired Gobert to put his own energy into becoming a better defender.

Gobert led the NBA in blocks in 2016–17, showcasing defensive skills that fit the mold of the D-first Utah Jazz. His wingspan and standing reach are downright ridiculous and off-the-charts long at 7-feet, 8 inches vertical. He can almost reach the basket without leaving his feet.

In 2018–19 Gobert was a beast on the boards, feasting on opponents who dared challenge him in the paint. He hauled down 25 rebounds in January versus the Detroit Pistons, outdueling Andre Drummond, a fellow traditional center and another problem underneath the glass. Gobert had 23 points and 22 boards the following game against the LA Clippers. He was also memorably ejected from a game just three minutes in against the Houston Rockets in December for yelling at the refs, the fastest toss of an NBA player in 15 seasons.

Gobert's been playing with one of the NBA's newest sensations, Donovan Mitchell, another underrated star who's been turning heads since his debut in 2017–18. Mitchell is a lights-out scorer, and with Gobert's skill set, the two have formed a one-two punch that's made Utah a threat once again in a stacked Western Conference, reminiscent of the team's glory days when John Stockton and Malone made the Jazz perennial contenders.

In 2018 Gobert was named Defensive Player of the Year for the first time, and the following season his stats were better than ever, especially on the offensive end. He was a double-double machine all season. He played 44 minutes in a double OT loss to the Oklahoma City Thunder, adding 26 points and 17 rebounds to his team's efforts. Late in the season, he scored 18 while adding 20 boards versus the Phoenix Suns.

He's been named to the All-Defensive First Team three seasons in a row, and he picked up his second Defensive Player of the Year award in 2019. He finished 2018–19 top five in rebounds, second in blocks and number one in field goal percentage (.669), while averaging nearly 16 points and 13 rebounds per game. It was more than just a breakout season — it was a revelation, one he and his mother saw coming years ago when he was a teen phenom in France. Now, across the planet, he's become known as a phenom on a global scale.

AL HORFORD 42

QUIETLY, ALMOST UNOBTRUSIVELY, Al Horford has become one of the best big men in the game, first helping propel the Atlanta Hawks from perennial first-round knock-out to one of the premier teams in the Association, and now plying his trade for the legendary Philadelphia 76ers.

Horford's quiet ascent may be because he hails from the Dominican Republic, a tiny island nation known primarily for producing baseball players. His father, however, played pro basketball for several years, and with his son's height and interest in the game, the elder Horford moved the family to Michigan when Al was 14 years old. At the All-Star Game in 2015 Horford remarked, "I fell in love with [basketball] real quick, watching my dad play."

Horford set myriad high school records before making the jump to college at the esteemed University of Florida. His move followed his father's footsteps, as Tito Horford suited up for the Miami Hurricanes in the late 1980s. The younger Horford made an immediate impact at Florida and, along with future NBA stars Corey Brewer and Joakim Noah, led the school during his sophomore and junior years to the NCAA Final Four title. The center entered the NBA as a two-time national champion, something very few players can say.

Drafted by Atlanta in 2007, Horford had a solid rookie year in 2007–08, putting up a respectable 10.1 points and 9.7 rebounds while averaging 31.4 minutes. He broke

out in his third season in the NBA, with a per-game line of 14.2 points, 9.9 boards and 79 percent shooting from the line. More impressively, he's maintained a career .525 field goal percentage over the course of his 12 years in the league, dipping below 50 percent from the floor just three times.

Horford's an old-school center: a classic pick-and-roll big man who can set screens for guards to attack the basket or look for

the open man. He's a strong presence on the back end and has been a leader both on and off the court. He's also dialed in from the midrange, possessing a sweet stroke defenders need to be wary of.

In 2014–15 Atlanta jumped out to a 35-8 start, putting together a 19-game winning streak and finishing 60-22 in the standings. Horford dropped his first career triple-double against the Philadelphia 76ers, recording

21 points, 10 rebounds and 10 assists during the Hawks' lengthy winning streak. Several days later he absolutely posterized Amir Johnson of the Toronto Raptors with a one-hand dunk after sidestepping Jonas Valanciunas. To cap off the month, he twice posted a double-double while adding three blocks. His smooth combination of skill, speed and athleticism makes him one of the most well-rounded centers in the game.

Horford finished the 2014–15 season averaging 15.2 points and 7.2 rebounds per contest (and put up almost identical stats the following year). His consistency continued in the playoffs, and he helped the Hawks to the third round for the first time in 35 years.

After a disappointing second-round exit at the hands of the Cleveland Cavaliers in 2015–16, Horford elected to become a free agent. In 2016 he signed a four-year, $113 million contract with Boston, where he helped lead the Celtics to the first spot in the Eastern Conference. In 2016–17 he averaged a steady 14 points, 6.8 boards and 5 assists a game, the latter a career high. He also hit a career-high 80 percent of his free throws in 2016–17.

Boston made it all the way to the Eastern Conference finals in 2017–18 thanks to the star power of Kyrie Irving and the dependable play of Horford, who averaged nearly 13 points, 4.7 assists and 7.4 rebounds in the regular season. After an exciting series versus Milwaukee and a near sweep of Philadelphia, Boston eventually faltered against LeBron James and the Cavs in seven games. Unabated, in 2018–19 Horford continued his trend of stellar play — in 68 games, he averaged 13.6 points and 6.7 rebounds per game while manning the middle for a Celtics squad that finished fourth in the east. He was efficient behind the three-point line and notched over 82 percent from the free-throw line. Boston swept Indiana in the first round of the playoffs but ran into the juggernaut that is Milwaukee, losing in five games to the number one team in

the Eastern Conference. Declining his player option with the Celtics for 2019–20, Horford decided to sign with division rivals Philadelphia in the 2019 off-season, penning a four-year, $109 million deal in the process.

Horford has fast become a household name, one of the greatest internationally born basketball players on the planet. And with his help, Philly appears to be a formidable threat to make deep playoff runs for years to come.

CAREER HIGHLIGHTS

- Named to NBA All-Rookie First Team in 2007–08
- Named to NBA All-Defensive Second Team in 2017–18
- Has played in five All-Star Games (2010, 2011, 2015, 2016, 2018)
- Was NBA Shooting Stars champion in 2011
- Named to All-NBA Third Team in 2010–11

SERGE IBAKA

THE FIRST NBA player from the Republic of Congo, Serge Ibaka rose to become the defensive force in the Oklahoma City Thunder's starting five before stops in Orlando and Toronto. And the 6-foot-10 power forward — who's a three-time All-Defensive First Team selection — is only getting better.

Ibaka may be Congolese, but he's multinational in terms of his citizenry. After cutting his teeth in the Spanish pro league, he loved the country so much he applied for citizenship. Once approved, he suited up for the Spanish national team, winning silver at the 2012 Olympics alongside the Gasol brothers.

Ibaka was selected by the Thunder (then the SuperSonics) with the 24th pick in the 2008 draft and debuted a year later as a 20-year-old in 2009–10. He saw limited action, suiting up for just over 18 minutes per game, and scored a respectable but unremarkable 6.3 points per game. His 5.4 rebounds per contest were stellar for his limited time on the floor, a strong indication of things to come.

The following season, Ibaka started 44 games, and his numbers increased accordingly, with per-game averages of 9.9 points, 7.6 boards and 2.4 blocks. With the three-headed attack of Kevin Durant, Russell Westbrook and James Harden, the Thunder went deep into the postseason, losing in the third round to the Dallas Mavericks. The run established Oklahoma as a perennial

playoff contender, and Ibaka proved to many that he was ready for the pressure of the big stage.

He arrived as a big-time defender in his third season. Ibaka led all players in total blocks (241) and blocks per game (3.7) in 2011–12 while adding a midrange jumper

to his offensive arsenal. In 2012–13 his well-rounded play had him leading all NBA players who attempted 300 or more shots from the midrange in field goal percentage. His former coach, Scott Brooks, called Ibaka "one of the best midrange shooters in the league," and he was right, as his numbers

- Named to NBA All-Defensive First Team three times (2011–12 to 2013–14)
- Ranks first in block percentage (5.8) among active NBA players
- Led the NBA in blocks twice (2011–12, 2012–13)
- Led the NBA in total blocks four times (2010–11 to 2013–14)
- Won an Olympic silver medal with the Spanish men's basketball team in London in 2012

was moved again, this time to Toronto. He finished the season averaging 14.8 points and 6.8 rebounds and added a dangerous three-point shot to his arsenal. In the 2017 off-season, he agreed to a three-year, $65 million deal to stay in Toronto and has since flourished north of the 49th parallel.

In 2018–19, Ibaka occupied several roles — starting center, backup center, power forward — and the Raptors big relished in it all. His patented shot from the elbow swished at will, and he put up respectable numbers: 15 points and 8.1 rebounds a game. The Raptors finished second in the Eastern Conference thanks in part to Ibaka's hard-nosed defense and offensive contributions, such as his 34 points and 10 boards versus the LA Lakers early in the season and his 25-point night versus the rival Milwaukee Bucks in January.

Ibaka saved his best work for deep in the Raptors' playoff run. He was instrumental in the final two series, providing much-needed muscle and heart in the Raptors' front court, culminating in the first championship ring of his career.

Ibaka has put in a lot of hard work, and it shows. Night in and night out, he sets up in the paint, patiently reading the post move of an opposing player, or he runs up the court, and instead of driving to the basket, he steps back, effortlessly for a big man, and hits nothing but net.

bested All-Stars Chris Paul and Marc Gasol. He again led the league in total blocks and blocks per game.

But 2014–15 was a difficult season for a Thunder team with championship aspirations. Durant missed 55 games, Westbrook missed 15, Ibaka missed 18 and the Thunder missed the playoffs. Ibaka still finished third in the league in blocks per game with 2.4, and despite a dip in his typically stellar field goal percentage, his offensive numbers weren't far off pace. Ibaka bucked the trend of shot-blockers being simply that; he is as well rounded a big as they come. "At that position, there are only a few guys

that can shoot that well," Westbrook said of his former teammate. In his final year in Oklahoma, Ibaka swatted away seven shots in a game versus Philadelphia, chipping in offensively with 11 points and 7 boards. Versus Golden State, he put up 15 points and hauled 20 balls off the glass. The team advanced to the Western Conference finals but fell to those same Warriors in seven games.

Soon after, Ibaka was traded to Orlando, where he shifted between center and power forward to combat the trend of smaller opposing lineups that toss up more threes. Midway through the 2016–17 season he

POSITION CENTER / **SHOOTS** RIGHT / **HEIGHT** 7'0" / **WEIGHT** 250 LB. / **DRAFTED** 2014, DENVER NUGGETS, 41ST OVERALL

NIKOLA JOKIC 15

NO ROOKIE FROM the 2015–16 NBA season made bigger strides than Serbian center Nikola Jokic, whose sophomore season caused a stir not only within the Denver Nuggets organization but all across the league. The big man made such an impact offensively that he's become the central force in the Rocky Mountain state.

Jokic finished third in rookie scoring in 2015–16, impressive for the 41st pick in the 2014 draft. The 7-foot, 250-pound center plays more like a guard. He has exceptionally soft hands and deft passing skills for a man who can easily shift between the 4 and the 5 positions on the court when called upon.

In February 2017, just days after Denver traded away fellow big Jusuf Nurkic, Jokic, with the frontcourt to himself, went off against the Golden State Warriors, dropping 17 points, 21 boards and 12 assists against a Warriors team that was coming off an emotional victory in Kevin Durant's first return to Oklahoma City. The Joker was grinning ear to ear. It was the first triple-double in NBA history with a shooting percentage of better than 50 percent. He then dropped an impressive 40 points at Madison Square Garden, which even on a good Sunday is a hostile environment for any visiting team. Those games opened everyone's eyes to the new face on the block.

To cap off that legendary February, the Serbian forward became the first Nuggets player to have back-to-back triple-doubles since Dikembe Mutombo — first against Chicago, when he put up 19 points, 16 boards and 10 dimes, and then versus the Bucks, when Jokic notched 13 points, 14 boards and 10 assists. The following night, for good measure, he scalded Charlotte for 31 points on 13-of-15 shooting.

If he's not hitting shots, Jokic's a dish-first big. If the passing lanes are cut off, he drives to the basket with authority. His vision on the court is lauded. And he has gotten better at being a physical presence on the glass.

He's a big who likes to dribble — he would have pretty much been a unicorn 10 years ago, but now, he's an extra threat for a team with strong outside shooting that includes up-and-coming Canadian Jamal Murray. Although Jokic finished his rookie season with admirable stats in just 22 minutes per game — 10 points, 7 rebounds, 2.4 helpers, a decent 81 percent from the free-throw line and 33 percent from behind the arc — his numbers in 2016–17 only improved, with him finishing with 16.8 points, 9.8 rebounds and 4.9 assists.

To say he's come of age quickly is an understatement. His meteoric rise beginning in the second half of 2016–17 was nothing short of amazing, and his numbers got even better in 2017–18, when he posted 18.5 points, 10.7 rebounds and 6.1 assists per game. The Nuggets just barely missed the playoffs, just one win behind the seventh and eighth positions in the Western Conference. Luckily for Denver fans, there was even more to come from the Serbian in 2018–19, when Denver finished second in the west and Jokic set career highs in all the major categories (20.1 points, 10.8 rebounds, 7.3 assists). He firmly established himself as the best passing center in the league and one of the hardest to guard. He showcased that skill set in the playoffs too, leading Denver to Game 7 of the second round, though the team would ultimately fall just short at the hands of Portland.

Jokic is prototypical of the new center in the NBA — naturally long and big, defensively responsible, strong under the rim and able to hit the occasional three. But what really separates him from the other bigs is his vision on the court, as evidenced by his high assist rate. In 2018–19, he ranked 6th in the league in assists with 580 helpers in the regular season.

Jokic will likely shift between the 4 and the 5 spots, providing options for the coaching staff depending on the matchup. It won't matter whom he guards, though — he'll be a handful for bigger centers because of his sleek passing and ball-handling skills, and power forwards will struggle with his big body and deft post moves. Wherever he is on the court, the Serbian makes his presence known, and after signing a five-year, $148 million contract in 2018, he's set to be a key presence on the Nuggets squad for years to come.

CAREER HIGHLIGHTS

- Named to NBA All-Rookie First Team in 2015–16
- Played in the 2019 NBA All-Star Game
- Named to All-NBA First Team in 2018–19
- Won an Olympic silver medal with the Serbian men's basketball team in Rio in 2016
- Won a silver medal at the 2013 FIBA World U19 Championship

POSITION POWER FORWARD / **SHOOTS** RIGHT / **HEIGHT** 7'3" / **WEIGHT** 240 LB. / **DRAFTED** 2015, NEW YORK KNICKS, 4TH OVERALL

KRISTAPS PORZINGIS 6

THERE WAS ONE bright light in an otherwise dim era for the once-storied New York Knicks, a team that failed to make the past six postseasons and continues its free fall from flagship franchise in the 1990s to current NBA whipping post. That bright light was hard to miss — a 7-foot-3 Latvian named Kristaps Porzingis.

The lanky power forward had an unusual journey to the NBA, skipping U.S. colleges and suiting up for CB Sevilla in the Spanish League as a teenager. He plugged away for several years in Spain, honing his game and getting bigger and stronger. Despite being eligible for the draft in 2014, Porzingis waited one more year to fill out. It paid off, and he was named the EuroCup Rising Star in 2015.

His tenure with the Knicks didn't begin well. Porzingis was widely booed on draft day by Knicks fans unfamiliar with the European. They thought they were getting another Euro big who would eventually become a bust, but little did they know the Latvian's skill set is one of a kind. Porzingis possesses guard quickness in a center's body, a willingness to take abuse under the rim and a dazzling array of ball skills. The fourth overall pick made an immediate impact in the NBA, ending his rookie season with 14.3 points per game, 7.3 rebounds and 1.9 blocks and giving Knicks fans a dash of hope.

Those hopes were shattered as the 2016–17 season began falling apart for the Knicks: former MVP Derrick Rose abruptly left the team before a home game to attend to a family matter back in Chicago, and Carmelo Anthony found himself in a Twitter war with then-Knicks executive Phil Jackson about the direction of the franchise. Trade rumors also dogged Melo as the team lost game after game to start 2017 and limped into the All-Star break with a 23-34 record. The tipping point arrived when Knicks legend Charles Oakley was arrested and thrown out of the arena on trumped-up charges that included disturbing the peace and trespassing. (Porzingis

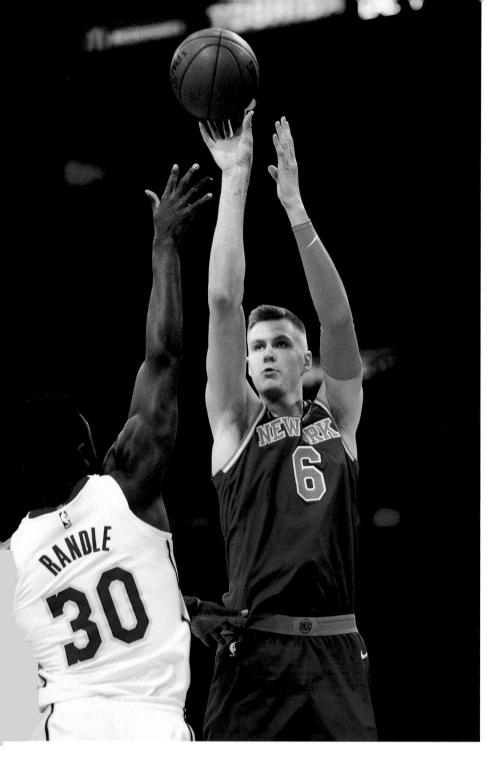

CAREER HIGHLIGHTS

- Named to NBA All-Rookie (First Team) in 2015–16
- Won the NBA All-Star Game Skills Challenge in 2017
- Finished second in Rookie of the Year voting in 2015–16
- Finished fifth in blocks per game (2.0) in 2016–17
- Named EuroCup Rising Star in 2015

Porzingis, but he finished strong once the drama in New York subsided. He also won the Skills Challenge at the All-Star break against some very talented guards, showcasing just how good he is for a man his size.

The 2017–18 season started off promising for the Latvian phenom. In November, he orchestrated an unforgettable comeback against the Indiana Pacers, notching 40 points, 8 rebounds and 6 blocks and pulling his team out of a 19-point deficit to win 108-101. He was selected as an All-Star Game reserve in January, but a season-ending torn ACL before the All-Star Weekend put an end to his breakout season. His stat line was no less remarkable: over 48 games he averaged 22.7 points, 2.4 assists and nearly 40 percent from three-point land.

Porzingis sat out the entire 2018–19 season with his injury, but the season wasn't without drama for the big man. He was traded midway through the year to the Dallas Mavericks, causing an uproar in the Big Apple as the fanbase felt the Knicks had traded away the team's best player. Dallas took a calculated risk taking on the injured Latvian, but it could pay dividends for years in Texas. Porzingis joins the flashy 2018–19 Rookie of the Year, Slovenian Luka Doncic. The two could form an international pair that will remind Mavs fans of the heady Nowitzki–Nash days. If that's the case, it's going to be a fun ride full of international flavor for years to come.

was quietly shooting free throws when the melee began.) This was all before the 2017 All-Star break, and the season shaped up to be a far cry from the 1990s when Oakley and Patrick Ewing were leading the Knicks deep into the playoffs year after year.

During his second NBA season, "Porzingod" finally figured out New York City. "I was getting caught up in traffic all the time," he joked in early 2017. For a big man, there's few like him. With unnatural length and a 240-pound frame, Porzingis is a force in the post. But his perimeter

game and behind-the-arc antics are unlike those of anyone his size. When he puts the two skill sets together, there's no stopping the power forward, and he explodes on the court. His sophomore numbers were solid — with increased minutes he shot the ball better from behind the three-point line and played a more important role in the Knicks offense. In December against the LA Lakers, he dropped 26 points, 13 boards and 7 blocks. The following night he lit up the Phoenix Suns for 34, going 4 for 4 from deep. Injuries in January hampered

PASCAL SIAKAM

43

THE TERM "UNICORN" gets bandied about often, but perhaps it most applies to Pascal Siakam, the Cameroonian power forward who plies his trade for the Toronto Raptors. After finishing his third season, this Swiss army knife of a player has established himself as one of the more unique athletes in the league and has fast become a cornerstone of the Raptors franchise.

Born in Douala, Cameroon, Siakam was selected 27th overall by Raptors president Masai Ujiri, a fellow African who saw him play at Basketball Without Borders in 2012. Siakam has three older brothers who all played college ball in the United States, but, ironically, the youngest and most successful of the four expressed no desire to play basketball, focusing instead on seminary school. Siakam was intelligent but lost interest in his studies and decided he didn't want to be a priest. On a whim he attended a free basketball camp set up by Houston Rockets forward Luc Mbah a Moute, another NBA player from Cameroon. Siakam was then invited to participate in Basketball Without Borders in South Africa, where Ujiri first saw him. Ujiri said to ESPN in 2017, "I will tell you honestly, when I saw Pascal in Basketball Without Borders, I couldn't even tell you if he was an NBA player." That's how raw Siakam was, but the potential was through the roof. He had an energy and relentlessness on the court that couldn't be taught and natural skills that didn't go unnoticed.

After attending prep school in Texas, Siakam spent two years at New Mexico State. In his final year, he averaged 20.3 points, 11.6 rebounds and over 2 blocks per game. He dedicated his college years to his father, whom he lost in a car accident in 2014, the day before his first college game. It was an earth-shattering moment that has fueled Siakam's rise in the NBA ever since.

Siakam started 38 games with the Raptors in his rookie year, but he was benched in January and then moved back and forth

between the NBA and the Raptors' G League team. In the G League he was able to get the playing time he itched for, averaging 29 minutes and 18 points a game and winning G League MVP after leading the Raptors 905 to the championship. Siakam's energy and work ethic started turning heads within the organization, and he became a permanent fixture on the NBA-level squad. In 2017–18, he became the focal point of the "bench mob" that dominated other teams' second units. He played 81 games that season, and the Raptors made it to the second round of the playoffs thanks in part to the bench's depth.

The 2018–19 season was Siakam's best to date. Before the start of the season, summer runs at UCLA polished his skills. It translated immediately on the NBA courts, and Siakam started every game but one. Per-game career highs in points (16.9), rebounds (6.9) and field goal, three-point and free-throw percentages (.549, .369 and .785, respectively) followed. In February 2019, he went off the charts, recording 33 points and 14 boards against Atlanta, then following that up with 44 and 10 versus Washington a week later. On both nights he shot 60 percent, and those double-doubles practically became par for the course all season long.

That success continued in the 2019 playoffs, when Siakam smoked the Orlando Magic for 30 points and 11 boards in 42 minutes in Game 3 and scored over 20 points in five of the seven games in the second-round series versus the Philadelphia 76ers. After struggling in Game 2 against the Milwaukee Bucks, Siakam went off in a double OT thriller the following game, playing over 51 minutes and adding 25 points and 11 boards.

Siakam arrived in the NBA Finals with a thud, dropping 32 in his finals debut and shocking the Golden State Warriors with his arsenal of moves. The Warriors had few answers for the league's most improved player, and the future looks bright for the budding superstar.

Siakam still thinks about his father often, saying, "There isn't a better man I've known in my life." With what he's accomplished in his career, especially during his breakout 2018–19 season, Siakam has undoubtedly made his pops proud. Whether he's spinning, jerking or running the floor with the speed of an antelope, you simply can't take your eyes off him. It's anybody's guess what's next for the Cameroonian forward who's taken the NBA by storm, but what's certain is he's bound to change the Raptors' fortunes for years to come.

CAREER HIGHLIGHTS

- Named NBA Most Improved Player in 2018–19
- Won the NBA G League championship in 2017
- Named NBA G League Finals MVP in 2017
- Named WAC Player of the Year in 2016
- Named WAC Rookie of the Year in 2015

ORLANDO MAGIC

POSITION CENTER / **SHOOTS** RIGHT / **HEIGHT** 7'0" / **WEIGHT** 260 LB. / **DRAFTED** 2011, PHILADELPHIA 76ERS, 16TH OVERALL

NIKOLA VUCEVIC ⁹

FROM THE TINY country of Montenegro hails a giant. The son of Yugoslavian basketball players, Nik Vucevic followed in their footsteps, eventually landing in the United States with a thud, all 7 feet of him. He's become a quiet, unheralded star who might be the NBA's most under-the-radar center.

He spent three years with the University of Southern California Trojans after moving to the States and was drafted 16th overall in 2011 by the Philadelphia 76ers. But his stock truly rose after the draft when he spent time during the 2011 NBA lockout playing in Europe. Scouts marveled at his length, rebounding and creative scoring.

In his final year at USC, Vucevic managed 17.1 points per game and 10.3 off the boards before declaring for the draft following his junior year of college.

He toiled for one year with the lowly Philadelphia franchise before a four-team, 12-player trade sent the European to the Orlando Magic, where he established himself as one of the most promising young big men in the NBA today.

When you're swapped in a deal that involves Dwight Howard, Andrew Bynum and Andre Iguodala, there's a lot to live up to. The weight was no problem for Vucevic. In January 2015, LA Clippers coach Doc Rivers called Vucevic "the best player in the league that nobody knows." Boston Celtics coach Brad Stevens went further, suggesting, "He may very well be an All-Star in the east at some point."

At 7 feet tall and 260 pounds, he's a quiet goliath, posting strong numbers throughout his career. Coaches have admired his ability to shoot the basketball and handle the ball in the post. He may not be a block-happy center on defense, but he makes up for that at the other end, using both hands to make sly moves in the post, or popping off the pick and roll and making his way to the basket, preferring "short rolls, the half-hook or half-floater," as Vucevic put it midway through 2014–15. Plus, he has shown steady improvement — in year one with Philadelphia, he started just 15 games, played in 51 and averaged just 5.5 points and 4.8 boards. At the end of his fourth year, Vucevic posted 19.3 points per game and 11 rebounds, and he put up a field goal percentage above .500. In 2018–19, as an eight-year vet, he started all 80 games he played, averaged 20.8 points and 12 rebounds, and maintained his field goal percentage at .518.

"Vooch" signed a four-year, $53 million deal with the Magic in 2014. He's enjoyed his time so much in Florida that he once claimed he wanted to be a member of the Magic for life. And why wouldn't Orlando want him? He's a double-double machine: in 2014–15 he amassed 45 double-doubles, which ranked him fourth highest in the league behind DeAndre Jordan, DeMarcus Cousins and Andre Drummond. He capped off the season with a 37-point, 17-rebound performance against the Minnesota Timberwolves on 18-of-25 shooting.

Vucevic has averaged a double-double in five of his eight seasons in the league and only seems to be bumping up his stat line as his career rolls on. He had his best season to date in 2018–19, and he recorded his second career triple-double in a match against the Philadelphia 76ers in October. With a new GM instated in 2017, Vucevic moved front and center as Orlando started turning things around. The Magic made the playoffs for the first time in a decade in 2018–19 thanks to the All-Star-level play of the man in the middle, who got his first All-Star Game nod as a reserve for Team Giannis in 2019.

Vucevic, alongside the Milwaukee Bucks' Nikola Mirotic, is making a name for Montenegrin basketball. Of the two Niks, it's Vucevic who could transform into a superstar. But the center will need to keep leading his team into the playoffs if he wants to follow in the mammoth steps of another big who made a name for himself in Orlando, Hall of Famer Shaquille O'Neal.

CAREER HIGHLIGHTS

- Played in the 2019 NBA All-Star Game
- Finished second in two-point field goals (629) in 2014–15
- Finished third in total rebounds (960) in 2018–19
- Is a two-time NBA Player of the Week
- Holds the Orlando Magic record for rebounds in one game (29)

CLUTCH PERFORMANCES

BASKETBALL IS REALLY quite simple. It's a quick, high-scoring game, with relentless up-and-down, back-and-forth action on the court. Twelve to a team. Five on the floor. Ten total. It's a sport played in two 24-minute halves and four 12-minute quarters. At times it's as complex as a high-screen pick and roll followed by a kick-out to the weak side for an open three, and sometimes it's simply one man versus another, mano a mano, with the clock winding down and nothing standing in the way but Father Time, a chance at immortality waiting.

Since James Naismith nailed two opposing peach baskets to the walls of a gymnasium in Springfield, Massachusetts, in 1891, the question of clutch has arisen in boardrooms and bars. Clutch is a measuring stick in the NBA by which men are judged and careers defined. In basketball, being clutch is everything.

There are clutch performers in every sport — the gunslinger QB in football, the shutdown goalie in hockey and the walk-off hitter in baseball. In basketball, clutch means a whole host of different things, but it is best encapsulated in one moment, one shot, one game, with everything on the line. Who emerges from the fray? Who, among the 10 men on the court, distinguishes himself in a league full of giants in a game that may be the last of the season? An athlete faces no greater test, no greater purpose, than rising to the challenge in the final minutes or seconds of a deciding game.

The Portland Trail Blazers' Damian Lillard, center, is mobbed by teammates after nailing a series-winning buzzer beater against the Houston Rockets in 2014.

IN RIP CITY! THERE'S NO TIME LIKE PLAYOFF TIME IN RI

Portland's Damian Lillard watches his series-winning shot against the Houston Rockets' Chandler Parsons in 2014. The shot sent the Trail Blazers into the second round of the playoffs for the first time in 14 years.

Clutch also happens to be susceptible to the way we choose to remember things. With so many seasons, so many players and so many incredible moments, it's hard to recall what happened when. What year? What team? What shot? And even though memory-making moments now emerge more readily thanks to instant replay and 24/7 sports channels, the moments etched in NBA lore are the ones we choose to remember best. It could be the player, the circumstance or the feat itself — but like most things in life, not all clutch moments are created equal.

Take Michael Jordan's push-off, fadeaway dagger over Byron Russell to seal the 1998 finals, or Larry Bird's steal with seconds left in the 1987 Eastern Conference finals against Isiah Thomas and the Detroit Pistons that won the Celtics the game. Every market has a franchise-defining moment. For the championship-starved Portland Trail Blazers, Damian Lillard's series clincher on home court in the first round of the 2013–14 playoffs versus the Houston Rockets wasn't just a series winner, it was history for the fans in Portland. Likewise for Toronto Raptors fans in the 2019 playoffs when Kawhi Leonard hit the first series-ending Game 7 buzzer beater in NBA

history, saving the Raptors' season. The ball bounced four heart-pounding times on the rim before sliding through the net, sending the Raptors into the third round. Leonard's shot avenged the 2001 second-round playoff loss to the same Philadelphia 76ers, when former Raptor Vince Carter clanked one off the rim.

But clutch moments also come in entire-game performances, not just instants in the waning moments of a game. Take Magic Johnson's Game 6 performance in the 1980 finals, where the rookie point guard started at center in lieu of Kareem Abdul-Jabbar and casually contributed 42 points, 15 boards and 7 assists while going 14 for 14 from the line in 47 minutes. In 2012, ESPN ranked Magic's night number two all-time for single-game performances. And don't forget the legendary Bill Russell's ridiculous 10-0 record in Game 7s, capped off by a 30-point, 40-rebound performance in 1962. Michael Jordan was so clutch he didn't even need a Game 7 in any of the finals he played in. He claimed MVP of the NBA Finals six times — that's called rising to the occasion on the biggest stage possible, over and over again.

With the advance of analytics, the definition of clutch is being rewritten, and the new math is contributing in a macro sense to a better understanding of a player's worth on the court. Perhaps, though, it's reducing the way we approach the micro — there's still something magical about that game-winning shot or jaw-dropping jam, even if it's seen in a six-second video on our smartphones. There's still something powerful about watching greatness explode off the dribble, perfection rising off the floor and magic floating toward the basket in slow motion.

The thrill of witnessing "clutch" manifest is bigger than victory itself. It doesn't matter if you don't remember the details. You'll remember how it made you feel: one man, one bucket, nothing but net.

THE SHOT

Poor Craig Ehlo. His Cleveland Cavaliers were a rising power in the Eastern Conference and had drawn the Chicago Bulls in the first round of the 1989 playoffs. It was Jordan's fifth NBA season, and the Bulls had never advanced past the first round since he'd arrived. Cleveland had finished 6-0 versus the Bulls that year in the regular season, finishing third to Chicago's sixth place. Cleveland was the clear favorite and Jordan and the Bulls the underdog.

In the final game of the best-of-five first round, with three seconds left on the clock, Jordan pushed through the screen, grabbed the inbounds pass and made toward the top of the key, a half step ahead of Ehlo. People forget Jordan wasn't a game-ending legend until that bucket in Game 5. From 15 feet he rose up to shoot. Ehlo jumped and reached up and flew by as Jordan hovered a moment longer than Ehlo could hang with him, and Jordan hit the rising shot over Ehlo's disappearing fingers as the clock hit zero and the Bulls clinched the series. The lasting image of Jordan jumping into the air, pumping his fist and beating his chest, is as famous as the shot that inspired the celebration.

Reggie Miller taunts New York Knicks celebrity fan Spike Lee after scoring 8 points in the final 18.7 seconds to steal Game 1 of the 1995 Eastern Conference semifinal.

Ehlo became so defined by Jordan's moment that when the former Cavs forward entered a rehab facility for addiction to painkillers following back surgery, a kid recognized him as the guy who was guarding Jordan. Some nights, some plays, some games, good or bad, define you. They follow you everywhere. They become part of the larger basketball narrative. Ehlo's last words before the inbounds — "Mr. Jordan, I can't let you score" — add drama to the story. Poor Craig Ehlo.

It says something when one of the most clutch moments in NBA history involves two players. When a basketball play becomes known as "the Shot," something has captured the imagination of basketball fans. Jordan's make, even though it didn't lead to a title that year, became the emotional hump the Bulls franchise needed to become NBA champions in 1991. Maybe that is why the Shot etched its way into the global consciousness.

As far as buzzer-beating, series-ending shots go, it's hard not to put the Shot up there as one of the greatest of all time. The Bulls would go on to beat the Cavs five times over a seven-year span in the playoffs. LeBron James and company exacted some revenge in 2015 by slaying the Chicago dragon that has so often breathed fire on the Cleveland basketball community.

REGGIE AT MSG

Sometimes it's not a playoff winning shot, though. It's more than that. It's a deep rivalry that pits one man against an entire city. That man is Reggie Miller, and the city? Where else but New York.

On May 7, 1995, nine seconds felt like a lifetime for Knicks fans. It was the Indiana Pacers. Reggie again. Reggie at Madison Square Garden again. The same Reggie who put up 25 in the fourth quarter of Game 5 in the 1994 conference finals the year prior, a ridiculous performance that drew the ire of fans from across all five boroughs. The same Reggie who returned to MSG to exact revenge for losing that series and missing a chance to compete in the 1994 NBA Finals. And it would be the same Reggie who, in Game 1 of the 1995 Eastern Conference finals, put a dagger through the hearts of New Yorkers that night in May, in just nine seconds, cementing his ruthless, road-killer persona for years to come.

Few NBA players ignited a firestorm in a road building like Miller. Film director Spike Lee sat courtside and provided the perfect people's champ — a passionate celebrity fan with New York street cred who lived and died with the Knicks.

The back-and-forth trash talk between spectator and player was a legendary sideshow to the Indiana–New York rivalry, providing a perfect backdrop for "Miller Time." The Knicks, up by six with 18.7 seconds to go in Game 1, held a seemingly impossible lead. But Miller came down the floor and coolly knocked down a three to cut the lead in half. The guard then improbably stole the ball off the inbounds, and in a moment of complete cold-blooded hubris, he backpedaled behind the arc instead of going for the easy layup that would have cut the lead to one. He drained it, tying the game. The Knicks' John Starks then missed two free throws at the other end, and Miller came back down the court, was fouled and ended up at

the line himself. In the span of nine seconds, the Knicks had gone from six points up to down by two, all in their home building at the hands of one man. Reggie.

As the buzzer sounded, Miller began mugging at Lee, grabbing his own neck. He yelled, "Choke artists!" while running into the tunnel following the robbery of Game 1, and the episode became immortalized in the 30 for 30 documentary entitled *Winner Time*. Time and time again, Miller saved his best for MSG — countless play-off performances that stunned the crowd and cemented a lifelong beef with Lee. Six playoff series over a span of seven years will do that. But it was those eight points in nine seconds in Game 1 of the 1995 Eastern Conference finals that everyone remembers as one of the deadliest clutch performances in NBA history.

LARRY BIRD

But sometimes clutch isn't just one game. It's a career's worth of highlights that define a player's clutch-worthiness. One such man is "the Hick from French Lick," Larry Bird.

Legendary not only for his shot but also for his trash talk, Bird was unassailable. He once told Xavier McDaniel exactly where he would be on the court after a time-out before hitting the game-winner. One evening, he hit a game-winning shot with Jordan, no slouch on D, right in his face. Upon winning his third three-point shootout in a row at the NBA All-Star Game, Bird's iconic finger was raised in the air as soon as the ball left his hands — he knew he'd won in a moment reminiscent of Babe Ruth's called shot. And of course there was the steal, probably the most famous steal of all time, when Bird snatched Isiah Thomas' inbounds pass, fed the ball to Dennis Johnson and won Game 5 of the 1987 Eastern Conference finals with his defense. He didn't just want to beat you — he wanted to destroy you, squeeze you into submission, ensure you cried on your way home because you couldn't contend with greatness.

Bird may not have as many game-winners on the highlight reel as other players, but he was iconically clutch, winning three NBA championships in the 1980s — twice named the finals MVP, three times in a row the regular-season MVP. There was a stretch in the 80s when he was simply unstoppable. In 1984–85, Bird did it all: 28.7 points a game, 10.5 rebounds, 6.6 assists and .427 from

three-point land. He was an 88 percent free-throw shooter, not even his career high. In his third-last year, at 34 years old, he shot 93 per-cent from the stripe, 21st all-time for one season, and he currently stands 11th all-time behind Reggie Miller. He didn't leave the league as a leader in any major categories, but his reputation was greater than that. Jordan, when asked once whom he'd pick to take the final shot, didn't hesitate: Larry Bird.

STEPH CURRY

If there's one player in the NBA currently holding the mantle for most clutch player in the league, it's not even close: Steph Curry. Yes, he's just crested 30. Yes, in recent years there have been more established superstars like Kobe and LeBron. But Kobe has retired and LeBron's catalog of buzzer beaters is thin, and a crop of young, big-time stars such as Curry is emerging around the league.

Stephen Curry, who scored 26 of his game-high 40 points after the start of the third quarter, celebrates Golden State's 123–119 overtime victory over the New Orleans Pelicans in Game 3 of their 2015 first-round series.

In his short tenure, Curry's past few seasons have proven he's the purest shooter in the NBA, the biggest threat from behind the arc and perhaps the least clutch-looking guy on the court with that mouth guard wagging from his lips. He's not tall — 6-foot-3 on a good day — and he's slight. Not skinny necessarily, just slight-looking. He's a favorite of the analytics crowd, too. Curry plays admirable defense for an offensive threat and a smaller guard, ranking high in SportVU and real plus–minus, and he finished first in steals in 2015–16. He also shot 886 three-pointers, making 402, ranking him first with just over a .630 shooting percentage despite hucking up 200-plus more shots than his teammate Klay Thompson that season. He demolished Reggie Miller's playoff record of 58 threes by launching 98 over the course of the Warriors' championship run in 2015, and he is already in the top five all-time for most threes made, and at one point he set the record for most made threes in one game — 13 (his teammate Klay Thompson took possession of that record in 2018–19 when he made 14 threes in one game).

Curry's deadly in the final seconds of a game. In Game 3 of the first round of the 2014–15 playoffs versus the New Orleans Pelicans, the Warriors, up two games but down 20 on the road in the fourth quarter, mounted an unimaginable comeback, conducted by none other than their maestro, Curry, whose fallaway three with seconds left sent the game into overtime. It was on the Internet before he could peel his body off the court. Curry hit the final two free throws for 40 points total to secure the win. (He finished with 39 the next game as they swept the Pelicans.) It was symbolic of everything clutch — despite a cold start, he caught fire at the end of a playoff game, knocking down bucket after bucket until the ultimate shot. He would be named regular-season MVP days later and would earn a second MVP honor the following season.

Kobe, LeBron, even Durant — keep 'em — Curry is the guy down one, down three, down 20 who gets the ball.

THE AGE OF ANALYTICS

The definition of clutch shooting is going through a transitional phase as analytics become a source of information to fans and GMs in an attempt to gather the true value of a player to his team. Video cameras are ubiquitous devices in NBA arenas these days — SportVU cameras in the rafters (used from 2013–14 until 2016–17) were installed to track every player's movement for the entire game. The technology the league has been using the past few seasons is called Second Spectrum, but the idea is the same. Sure, coaches still scratch Xs and Os on the sidelines during a time-out. But the real work is being done in dark rooms, far beyond the reaches of the

Chris Paul steals the ball from LA's Nick Young in 2014–15. Paul led the NBA in steals that season; it was his sixth time leading the league in the stat.

or real plus–minus, is another stat gaining momentum on ESPN. In 2015 Dallas Mavericks owner Mark Cuban told ESPN that "Analytics have been an important part of who we are since I walked in the door 15 years ago. We have strived to introduce new and exclusive sources of data so that we can improve performance of our players." Those PhDs are even introducing papers that attempt to explain defensive worth on the basketball court, tracking and analyzing "counterpoints," which, according to now-shuttered Grantland, "estimate how many points an individual defender allows per 100 possessions."

In 2015 Alexander Franks and Andrew Miller, the authors of the study, suggested Chris Paul was the top defensive point guard in the league after crunching the numbers. Although it seems obvious to the naked eye that Paul is pretty money without the ball, the numbers backed it up, and we entered territory that the assistant vice president of Stats LLC called "the ability to measure the impact individual defenders are having throughout the game," a huge leap forward for the NBA. Paul's reputation as a winner had taken a hit over his career, thanks to few playoff series wins. That changed when Paul willed the Clippers past the reigning-champion San Antonio Spurs in a thrilling Game 7 victory in the first round of the 2015 playoffs, and his game-ending shot, off-balance with Tim Duncan's hand in his face, silenced his critics. The point is: it's easy to see Paul's worth when he nets a series winner. Those SportVU cameras recorded not only where Paul was on the court, and the two points that counted on the scoreboard, but also how he fared throughout the game. Beyond well-known players like Paul, general managers can use advanced statistics to identify undervalued players who add an element to the game beyond baskets.

Several GMs now come from an analytics background, including Houston Rockets head honcho Daryl Morey. The Rockets were the first team in the NBA to hire a cadre of stats guys in the front office to give them an edge. On the court, the team is led by James Harden, and the Rockets have all but eliminated a midrange jump shot from their offensive attack, taking an inordinate number of threes or shots in the paint not only because the stats back it up but also because the assembled personnel provide a reason to. If Harden or any of his backcourt counterparts miss one of their umpteen threes — they led the league in attempts in 2017 and set an NBA record for most made threes in one game in 2019 — the team is ready to gobble up the board by committee. In 2016–17 Houston finished in the top 10 for

court, where data gets sent from those cameras. Statisticians and newly hired data analysts then review mountains of data. It's complicated stuff — most stats guys are professors or PhD students in economics and do not come from a sports background. But they're massive basketball pioneers on the frontier of applying science to the hardcourt.

Shooting charts are growing in popularity and are easily available online. Phrases like "expected performance value," or EPV, are creeping into the casual fan's vocabulary, and stats like PER (player efficiency rating) and true shooting percentage are already mainstream on sites like basketball-reference.com. Adjusted plus–minus,

the realm where a player's complete skill set comes into play over a longer period of time. Quantifying stats may not be the sexiest way to understand a basketball player's worth, but it's growing in popularity. At the very least, for stats geeks around the world, it's provided an arsenal for debate at the bar when Harden pulls up for another three, or a lanky center settles for a long-range jack instead of attacking the rim.

The way we understand the game has certainly changed, and players like Harden and Russell Westbrook are being coveted in the draft. As a point guard coming out of college, Westbrook had his size and assist rate challenged. But Seattle/Oklahoma's brass saw an opportunity, and after his MVP-winning season in 2016–17 and his consecutive seasons averaging triple-doubles, the Thunder management and their analytics team look like geniuses in identifying Westbrook's superstar talent.

There will always be obvious choices every draft. Victor Oladipo and Andrew Wiggins were automatic top-two selections in the 2013 and 2014 drafts and immediate everyday NBA players. So were Karl-Anthony Towns and D'Angelo Russell, the number one and two overall selections in 2015. The trick is using analytics to go further. It's those teams at five through 10 who should be using everything available to make value judgments on future NBA players.

Houston Rockets guard James Harden, the darling of the analytics movement, scores on a fast break layup against the Washington Wizards.

total rebounds without an elite rebounder.

Not everyone, however, has embraced the new era of statistical data. In 2015 Charles Barkley called Morey "one of those idiots who believes in analytics." That season, the Lakers, Knicks and Nets had been well behind the eight ball in embracing the philosophy of numbers, and the Knicks and Lakers — unsurprisingly based on the advanced statistics — finished in the top five of field goal attempts made from 15 to 19 feet that year. In other words, they took a lot of poor probability midrange shots. The Rockets? They were dead last in this category.

So what does it say about the way we're understanding clutch? Maybe we're moving past the highlight-reel buzzer beater into

WE'VE COME A long way since Mr. Naismith, in that old gymnasium in 1891, recalled a game from his Canadian childhood named "Duck on a Rock" and went about creating the rules for a new game he'd call "Basket Ball." From no backboards and a closed hoop, we've arrived at a time and place that includes dozens of in-arena cameras, optical tracking systems and the uber-analysis of the game at a second-by-second level. It's impossible to think what Naismith would have thought about all this technology. It doesn't mean that anything has irrevocably changed since Naismith wrote his first 13 rules — the game is fundamentally the same. There are still 10 men on the court, five a side, with the goal to put the ball in the opponent's basket. And what will never go away is that last-minute shot, the anticipation as the clock ticks down that one man is getting the ball and one man is defending him. One of them will walk off the court, head shaking. The other, arms raised, a hero.

DEANDRE AYTON

POSITION CENTER / SHOOTS RIGHT / HEIGHT 7'1" / WEIGHT 250 LB. / DRAFTED 2018, PHOENIX SUNS, 1ST OVERALL

DEANDRE AYTON 22

THERE'S PLENTY OF pressure when you're the number one pick in the NBA Draft. That's the position Deandre Ayton found himself in, the starting center for the Phoenix Suns and an athletic phenom who has dominated at every level of play. Now, it's up to the 7-foot-1, 250-pound big man to continue rising to the occasion.

The Suns are a team in the midst of a major rebuild. With budding superstar Devin Booker as one of the team's cornerstones, they turned to the Bahamian-born big who set his sights on the NBA early. Playing high school ball in San Diego and later Phoenix, Ayton immediately grabbed the attention of scouts, thanks to his freakish combo of size and athleticism. His skills were raw; his enthusiasm and will to get better were off the charts. Following his one-and-done year at the University of Arizona, he racked up a laundry list of awards, including being named to the NCAA AP All-America First Team and winning the Pac-12 Conference Player of the Year award and the Karl Malone Award, given to the top college-level power forward.

Born in Nassau, the capital of the Bahamas, Ayton follows in the tradition of Mychal Thompson, a former number one pick, the father of Klay Thompson and the first NBA player from the island nation. So when Ayton was announced as the Suns' first selection in the 2018 draft, you can bet the entire country was watching. It was a long way from the basketball camps Ayton paid for out of his own pocket (working as a plumber alongside his step-dad). When Ayton returned home following the draft, a hero's welcome greeted the boy who had managed to stay out of trouble in his rough neighborhood thanks to supportive parents who built a basketball hoop in front of their house. Kids swarmed Ayton when he made an appearance at the same camp he once attended. The prime minister called him "the son of the soil" when the future NBA star visited the parliament.

Ayton is fresh in the league and his game is still growing. But there were definite highlights from his rookie season that stood out just as much as his 7-foot-1 frame. He posted six double-doubles in his first 10 games, including a 17-point, 18-rebound effort on the road against the Toronto Raptors. He put up 23 and 18 against the Boston Celtics,

CAREER HIGHLIGHTS

- Named to NBA All-Rookie First Team in 2018–19
- Finished 10th in field goal percentage (.585) in 2018–19
- Participated in the Rising Stars Challenge in 2019 for Team World
- Named Pac-12 Player of the Year for 2017–18
- Won the Karl Malone Award in 2018

Nash won back-to-back MVPs and the Suns were perennial Western Conference contenders.

Ayton has other skills to work on, notably adding a three-pointer to his arsenal, something most big men now possess in spades, and improving his defensive game, which takes years to learn. He'll also need to shed the image of being the wrong pick — Dallas Mavericks shooting guard and third overall pick Luka Doncic took the NBA by storm in 2018–19. Although hindsight is 20/20, Ayton's season paled in comparison. To his credit, the Suns managed to pick up some Ws in March — Ayton contributed several double-doubles, including 26 points, 10 boards and 10-of-14 shooting from the free-throw line against the LA Lakers — but there's still a ways to go if he wants to make a big impact on the league and bring greatness back to the desert.

Make no bones about it: the Suns were bad in 2018–19, and they finished with a 19-63 record. But Ayton was a bright star in a murky galaxy. In his first full season, he averaged 16 points, 10 rebounds and 30 minutes a game. Now he and Booker are the cornerstones of a franchise waiting for one more piece to fit the puzzle, and the 2019 draft is loaded with talent.

As Tom Petty once sang, "the waiting is the hardest part."

another Eastern Conference contender, in mid-December before going off for 33 points and 14 rebounds after Christmas versus the Denver Nuggets.

The budding star can score and rebound, that's for sure. But despite his physique, he still needs to build some bulk to compete with the biggest centers in the league. The hope is that Booker and Ayton will perfect the pick and roll much the same way former Phoenix stars Steve Nash and Amar'e Stoudemire did in the early 2000s, when

POSITION SHOOTING GUARD / SHOOTS RIGHT / HEIGHT 6'6" / WEIGHT 210 LB. / DRAFTED 2015, PHOENIX SUNS, 13TH OVERALL

DEVIN BOOKER 1

YOU MAY HAVE seen it. Maybe you heard about it the next day on ESPN. The night Devin Booker went off for 70. It was March 24, 2017, during the shooting guard's sophomore season, but it seems like yesterday because it's seared in our collective memories. That game showed us there's more to come from the Phoenix Suns' franchise player.

Booker lived a nomadic life in high school, starting first in Grand Rapids, Michigan, with his mom and then moving to Mississippi to live with his father, Melvin Booker, a former college ball player at Missouri turned semi-pro baller turned high school teacher. His star pupil was his son Devin. The shooting guard dominated high school — he averaged a whopping 30.9 points per game his senior year— and scholarships were handed out like candy at Halloween. Booker chose Kentucky and played with six other players who were all drafted in the 2015 class. Although the team lost in the semifinals of the NCAA tournament, they rang up 38 straight wins along the way. Booker, who didn't even start as a freshman, was taken 13th overall by the Suns.

In his rookie season Booker was the Suns' leading scorer and was named to the NBA All-Rookie First Team, finishing fourth in Rookie of the Year voting. He turned heads midway through the season when he dropped 32 against the Indiana Pacers, making six threes. Against Miami several months later, he recorded 34 points on the scoresheet — a feat he repeated later in the season, showing he was no flash in the pan. The Suns went 23-59 in 2015–16, but they knew they had their man.

In his second season, the year he dropped 70, Booker was a night-in, night-out stat-stuffer. He notched 22.1 points per game and over 36 percent from three-point land while averaging 35 minutes and starting every game he played. In the sixth and seventh games of the season, he dropped 38 and 39, respectively, signaling to the league he was ready to take it to the next level. He scored 39 in back-to-back games in January before his 70 points late in the season versus the Boston Celtics.

Even the notoriously loyal Boston crowd cheered him on that night — one for the history books. Booker was on the road, so

CAREER HIGHLIGHTS

- Named to NBA All-Rookie First Team in 2015–16
- Won the NBA Three-Point Contest in 2018
- Finished seventh in points per game (26.6) in 2018–19
- Finished seventh in minutes per game (35.0) in 2018–19
- Named SEC Sixth Man of the Year in 2015

the spotlight was bright. His effort represented the most points in a game the league had seen since Kobe Bryant's 81 against Toronto in 2006. Booker was the youngest to ever put up that kind of stat line, and to top it off he shot 24 of 26 from the stripe. Others in the 70-plus club include greats such as Elgin Baylor and Wilt Chamberlain.

Booker's totals increased his third year in the league — 24.9 a game and 88 percent from the line, and his assist and rebound numbers inched their way up — punctuated by a 46-point, 8-rebound game versus Philadelphia in December and a gaudy 43-6-8 line against Portland in January. But an injury late in the season derailed him, and he played only 54 games in 2017–18. The Suns won just twice in their last 27 games.

The addition of 2018 number one pick Deandre Ayton didn't detract any from Booker's numbers in 2018–19. He regularly hit 38 points despite battling injuries. He even dropped 41 against the New York Knicks, beat LeBron James and his new LA Lakers, and defeated Steph Curry and his cohorts in Oakland (stopping an 18-game losing streak for his franchise) as the Suns started to show signs of life in early March. To emphasize that he is a force to be reckoned with, Booker scored 59 points in late

March and then followed up with another 50, becoming the youngest player ever to post back-to-back 50-point games.

Despite the effort on the part of their star, the team stayed mired in the basement like a surly teenager. No bother — Booker's ultra-committed to the Phoenix area and has already dug deep roots in the community, embracing his Latin heritage (his mother is Mexican American and Puerto Rican), which much of the fanbase shares, and befriending one local fan with special

needs — something he embraces since his sister is also developmentally challenged. He's exactly the guy you want as a franchise cornerstone, and he signed a five-year, $158 million contract in 2018, meaning he's around for the long haul.

He is one of the NBA's greatest scoring threats, and for basketball fans in the desert longing for a return to the playoffs, they know who is going to get the ball when the clock ticks down. It's not a matter of if, it's when.

POSITION POINT GUARD / SHOOTS LEFT / HEIGHT 6'3" / WEIGHT 175 LB. / DRAFTED 2017, SACRAMENTO KINGS, 5TH OVERALL

DE'AARON FOX ⑤

ACCORDING TO THE comic books, the fastest man alive is named Barry Allen, aka the Flash. But you'd forgive De'Aaron Fox for thinking he can lay claim to the title. In seconds, Fox blows by the competition, and if he isn't the Flash, he's certainly one of the quickest players on the basketball court we've seen in years.

Drafted fifth overall in 2017 by the Sacramento Kings, Fox has flourished in his first two seasons in the NBA. The University of Kentucky product was a standout in college — he scored 39 points in the Elite Eight and was regarded as one of the top point guards in the country. He played just one season because he was NBA ready, scoring 16.7 a game and dishing out 4.6 assists in his only college campaign.

Fox grew up in the Houston, Texas, area, and during his high school days he put up 50 points twice. He committed to play at Kentucky after wowing scouts at the Jordan Brand Classic and the Nike Hoop Summit, and he continued turning heads when he flashed his skills in college. The only question was how high he would go on draft day — Fox himself believed he should have been drafted in the top three, and some teams might be kicking themselves for not believing the same. "I play the hardest," he said just days before the draft. It's no surprise his favorite player growing up was Kevin Garnett, another hardworking, ultra-competitive NBA player.

In his rookie year Fox put up 11.6 points and 4.4 assists per game and clocked nearly 28 minutes a night while playing starting point guard for a Kings team rebuilding around their new, flashy court general. He scored a season-high 26 points versus San Antonio, going 6 for 6 from behind the arc. The Kings may have missed the playoffs, but hope abounded, and several key additions and subtractions — notably DeMarcus Cousins — changed the makeup of the Sacramento team headed by former '90s star Vlade Divac.

Fox's sophomore campaign was his coming-out party. Starting 81 games, he put up 17.3 points and 7.3 assists (good for eighth in the league) and shot 37 percent

Fox makes his opponents reel back when he blows by them with a burst of speed. He's claimed he's faster than superstars Russell Westbrook and John Wall, the latter considered the fastest man in the league from line to line. Fox's (and Wall's) college coach, John Calipari, agrees with the younger point guard that he's number one in the quickness department. In a short time, defenders have become acutely aware of Fox's speed. But it's not just his speed that catches opponents off guard — as with any point guard, his high basketball IQ is the bread and butter of his arsenal, and that court awareness has already made him into a top-10 assist maker in the NBA. When he is putting up stats like 30 and 12 against the Cleveland Cavs, or 28 points and 12 assists like he did versus the Oklahoma City Thunder in December — well, he's showing that he's basically the engine and the steering wheel of the Kings offense. With potential future stars in fellow former lottery picks Buddy Hield, Marvin Bagley Jr. and Willie Cauley-Stein, the Kings may have hit the jackpot of lineups. But make no mistake — Fox is the straw that stirs this protein shake.

Off the court, Fox is a video game enthusiast, renowned for his elite gaming abilities as well as a stubborn, refuse-to-lose attitude. He also loves breakfast foods and is an amicable personality, already taking the initiative to set up charity programs back in his hometown of Houston.

Good news for Central California fans — Sacramento has turned a corner from the Cousins era, and Fox may be the new captain that the long-sinking Kings need to resurrect themselves from the murky waters of mediocrity. He's so fast, you won't even know it's happened until the buzzer sounds and his ship rises from the depths.

CAREER HIGHLIGHTS

- Finished fourth in assists (590) in 2018–19
- Finished sixth in steals (133) in 2018–19
- Finished eighth in assists per game (7.3) in 2018–19
- Named SEC Tournament MVP in 2017
- Named to All-SEC First Team in 2016–17

from behind the arc. In just the first month of the season, Fox registered his first triple-double — 31-10-15. He followed that up with 15 points, 12 dimes and 9 boards against the LA Lakers. By the final month of the 2018–19 season, he averaged 33 minutes a game and dropped 30 points on the hapless New York Knicks.

CHICAGO BULLS

POSITION POINT GUARD–SHOOTING GUARD / **SHOOTS** RIGHT / **HEIGHT** 6'5" / **WEIGHT** 200 LB. / **DRAFTED** 2014, MINNESOTA TIMBERWOLVES, 13TH OVERALL

ZACH LAVINE 8

ZACH LAVINE MAY have gone unnoticed at the start of his career as the Minnesota Timberwolves freshman not named Wiggins, but ever since his high-flying antics at both the 2015 and 2016 NBA All-Star Games, LaVine has proven he's one to watch. Now he's playing for the Chicago Bulls and looking to help turn around the fortunes of the franchise made famous by the legendary Michael Jordan.

At 6-foot-5 and 200 pounds, the guard doesn't cut an imposing figure, but his talent level is off the charts. When the Wolves drafted him they needed athleticism and coveted the UCLA product. What they got by selecting LaVine 13th overall was a multiposition guard who is proving he possesses a higher ceiling than people may have thought.

One of Washington state's best high school players, LaVine jumped to the college scene, suiting up for the UCLA Bruins. He lasted only a year and wasn't even one of the best players on the team. But, boy, the kid could dunk (he sports a rumored one-step 46-inch vertical).

"Thank God for the Internet" must have been what every basketball fan muttered when LaVine showed up at the 2015 Slam Dunk Contest. Inside the Barclay's Center in Brooklyn, LaVine could not have picked a better or bigger arena to showcase his bag of tricks. Wearing the "Toon Squad" No. 23 jersey from the movie *Space Jam* — an homage to Michael Jordan — LaVine

entered the arena to the theme song from the movie. It was nothing if not hubristic, but the kid from Washington walked the walk, demolishing the competition.

His first dunk: between the legs. His second: behind the back. Both spectacular.

LaVine had the crowd and a crew of NBA superstars on the sidelines jumping out of their seats. It was the most exciting dunk contest since Vince Carter brought the house down in 2000, and it has helped elevate LaVine's status around the league.

LaVine had many highlights that year outside the Slam Dunk Contest. In November 2014, he poured in 28 versus Kobe Bryant and the LA Lakers. In April 2015 versus the top-seeded Golden State Warriors, LaVine went off for 37 points, knocking down 6 of 10 threes on 13-of-21 shooting from the field, and adding 9 boards and 4 helpers. He finished his rookie season with 10.1 points, 3.6 assists and 2.8 rebounds, a solid contributor who was rewarded with increased playing time as the year went on. When point guard Ricky Rubio was lost to injury, LaVine gobbled up the minutes, playing out of his usual position but not looking out of position. He ranked second in rookie free-throw percentage, fifth in rookie scoring and eighth in rookie shooting percentage from behind the arc.

In 2015–16, LaVine continued to get better, playing all 82 games and averaging 14 points a contest. His 35 points off the bench — on 14-of-17 shooting, no less — versus the Oklahoma City Thunder was an overture for the real symphony of the season: his head-to-head battle with Aaron Gordon in the 2016 Slam Dunk Contest. The competition required max effort from both the reigning champ and the eventual runner-up. With the crowd jumping out of their seats every time Gordon or LaVine threw it down — like LaVine's balletic flight to the hoop from just before the foul line — their performances were modern-day opuses for dunk enthusiasts.

LaVine started the 2016–17 season well, averaging 18.9 points and three assists, but an ACL injury landed him on the sidelines halfway through the campaign. In June 2017, in a blockbuster draft-day deal, LaVine, Timberwolves teammate Kris Dunn and the seventh overall pick, Lauri Markkanen, were traded to the Chicago Bulls for Jimmy Butler and the 16th pick, Justin Patton.

LaVine played only 24 games in 2017–18, but in 2018–19 he came back fired up and healthy, finishing 16th in NBA scoring with 23.7 points a game, despite playing on a rebuilding Bulls team that went a meagre 22-60. The season was punctuated by LaVine's 42 points versus the Boston Celtics in February and a 47-9-9 line in a quadruple OT thriller versus the Atlanta Hawks, in which the guard played a whopping 56 minutes. It's safe to say the left knee is fine, although the Bulls did end LaVine's season early after he developed soreness in his right knee.

Chicago is looking to set a new direction for its team with their crop of young talent, including a top first-round draft pick in 2019. As long as he stays healthy, LaVine will have the opportunity to keep growing as a star and potentially define a new path for the storied Bulls franchise.

POSITION SHOOTING GUARD / **SHOOTS** RIGHT / **HEIGHT** 6'3" / **WEIGHT** 215 LB. / **DRAFTED** 2017, DENVER NUGGETS, 13TH OVERALL

DONOVAN MITCHELL 45

IT'S SAFE TO say no one thought Donovan Mitchell had it in him. He wasn't a top-five pick in the draft. He landed in Utah, not exactly considered the epicenter of basketball. What fans in Salt Lake City got was a sleeping giant, a diamond in the rough who took the league by storm in 2017–18 during his rookie year and delivered again in his sophomore campaign, proving it was no fluke.

The 13th overall pick in the 2017 draft, Mitchell was selected by the Nuggets and traded on draft night to the Jazz. The Louisville product played two seasons of college ball, averaging 15.6 points in his sophomore year. He was a bright light in college and can still be seen donning Cardinal red in the off-season or on the custom shoes he wore in his NBA rookie season.

Mitchell grew up just outside of New York City, in Elmsford. His father works for baseball's New York Mets. But the younger Mitchell was a budding baller, and he attended prep schools in New Hampshire and Connecticut before heading to the University of Louisville on a scholarship. His mother, a teacher, ensured Mitchell never neglected his studies — she held him back from a game in eighth grade because he hadn't memorized an assignment, something that stuck with Mitchell as he ascended the basketball ranks — and he became a star student both in the classroom and on the court, known for his

fastidiousness and dedication to learning and improving. He's even going to finish his degree while playing in the NBA — he promised his mom he would.

Mitchell's rookie season was one to behold. He went toe to toe with Ben Simmons all season for the Rookie of the Year title, and their rivalry was a major

storyline throughout 2017–18, with Mitchell calling into question Simmons' eligibility (the Aussie missed an entire season after being drafted because of an injury). Mitchell put up 20.5 points per game, 3.7 boards and 3.7 assists; he shot a respectable 34 percent from behind the arc and 80 percent from the free-throw line. But it was his penchant for pizzazz and clutch shots that made him a household name in his first season. When he threw up 41 points in December 2017, fans took notice. He registered another 40-point game two months later in early February versus Phoenix, making an impression on the NBA's elite players. Then he punctuated it all by winning the Slam Dunk Contest.

Utah made the playoffs, and Mitchell took over. He set several rookie scoring records and dropped 38 on the Oklahoma City Thunder in Game 6 to clinch the first round, despite playing on a hobbled foot he injured in Game 2. The Jazz lost to the Houston Rockets in the second round, but the postseason signaled a new star was on the rise. Gone were the days of Gordon Hayward; now Mitchell and rising star center Rudy Gobert are the talk of the team. Although he didn't win Rookie of the Year — Simmons edged him — Mitchell clearly made his mark.

The 2018–19 season was much the same — Mitchell was steady, scoring at a similar clip. The Jazz stayed in the mix in a tough Western Conference, finishing 50-32 en route to the playoffs. Mitchell put up some heady numbers along the way: 38 against the Memphis Grizzlies and back-to-back 30-point games versus the New York Knicks and the Atlanta Hawks. And, oh yeah, how about that 46 he dropped in a 115-111 win against the Milwaukee Bucks, the best team in the league in 2018–19? Mitchell finished the season averaging nearly 24 points a game, 80 percent from the stripe, and 36 percent from three-point land. But Utah's postseason ended swiftly. The team bowed out in the first round of the playoffs to the Houston Rockets, despite Mitchell's 21 points per game, including 34 in Game 3 in Utah's only win.

The shooting guard has also made his mark off the court, gifting his fourth-grade teacher's daughter a $25,000 scholarship. Clearly he hasn't forgotten how important education was in his own life.

Now that Utah has unearthed its diamond in the rough, the sky's the limit for an organization that once flourished with the one-two punch of Karl Malone and John Stockton — two of the NBA's modern all-time greats. Mitchell now has a chance to become another low-key, gracious star in Utah who inspires both on the court and off. Mitchell has been quietly rising ever since he started dribbling a ball, so the question is, where is his ceiling? It appears he keeps touching it wherever he goes.

POSITION POINT GUARD–SHOOTING GUARD / **SHOOTS** RIGHT / **HEIGHT** 6'4" / **WEIGHT** 207 LB. / **DRAFTED** 2016, DENVER NUGGETS, 7TH OVERALL

JAMAL MURRAY

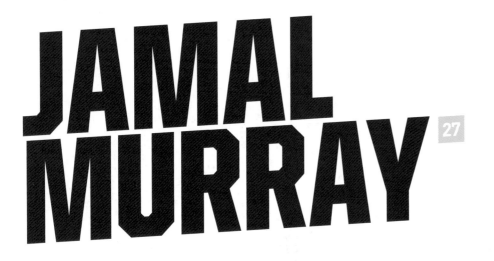

IT DIDN'T TAKE long for Jamal Murray to insert himself into the conversation of best Canadian basketball players in the NBA. Following in the footsteps of former MVP Steve Nash and current Minnesota star Andrew Wiggins, Murray, in just his third year in the league, had the best campaign of his career. The point guard from Kitchener, Ontario, led the Nuggets to their best season in years and is poised to break out as the guard to watch.

He can thank his dad for the work ethic. Murray's dad made his 7-year-old son hit 30 free throws in a row before he could leave the court, and Murray learned to shoot outside in the biting Canadian winters. Now that's hardcore. Meditation and martial arts also provided mental lessons that Murray exhibits on the court — play through pain, challenge yourself to be the best and find your inner calm, something he learned while jacking threes in a snowstorm.

The Canadian kid was drafted seventh overall by Denver after a standout season at University of Kentucky. He shot 95 percent from the free-throw line his freshman year and averaged 20 points per game. In a January 2019 article, his former coach, John Calipari, told ESPN, "Jamal's got a little chip on his shoulder" with regard to how he's perceived as he tries to assert his position among the NBA greats. It has translated into on-court beefs with high-profile superstars, such as Kyrie Irving. Murray insists "it's nothing personal," but for better or worse,

CAREER HIGHLIGHTS

- Named to NBA All-Rookie Second Team in 2016–17
- Finished fifth in free-throw percentage (.905) in 2017–18
- Named Rookie of the Month for November 2016
- Named to All-SEC First Team in 2015–16
- Named to NCAA AP All-America Third Team in 2015–16

he has drawn the ire of opposing players because of his competitive spirit.

In his second season, he shot over 90 percent from the free-throw line and 38 percent from behind the arc. His 2018–19 numbers in those categories may have fallen a touch, but his scoring is up, at just over 18 points for the season. Rather than stats, it's Murray's magical nights that stand out. How about his 48 points against the Boston Celtics in early November 2018,

remembered more because Murray tried to huck up a three at the end of the game to make over 50? That drew the indignation of Boston's players, who felt it was against the code of conduct because Denver had the game wrapped. Or how about Murray's 22 points, 15 dimes and 7 rebounds versus the Dallas Mavericks in December? Or one more for good measure: the 46-point effort after Christmas versus the Phoenix Suns, in which Murray added 8 assists and 6 boards to boot. He also hit some memorable buzzer beaters in 2018–19, including a half-court shot to end the first quarter against Golden State that drew national attention the next morning. It speaks to his no-fear mentality. Murray will shoot from everywhere. His teammate Malik Beasley put it this way: "Jamal thinks every one of his shots is going to go in."

The 6-foot-4, 207-pound guard is a handful. Quick, with a shoot-first mentality, he forces defenders to give him space or he'll burn them off the dribble. If not that, he'll

just stop on a dime and pull up for a quick jumper below the rim. He has morphed into a two-headed dragon alongside Nikola Jokic — one of the best passing big men in the game — and the future looks bright in the Rockies. If there's one knock on the guard, it's consistency, but Murray's figuring out how to be less streaky. What he has established is a reputation, which counts for a lot: hard to play against, in your face, won't back down or, as some writers have called him, a "heel," to use a wrestling term. He almost enjoys being disliked, or at least, he revels in pissing off his opponents. As long as he's putting up 20 points a game and Denver is winning, it seems Murray is content.

He's found a home in Denver — a long way from Kitchener, Ontario — and made a name for himself as one of the up-and-coming stars in the NBA. Self-belief and discipline don't appear to be a problem. Murray often says he believes he possesses a "mental edge" on the competition. Will it translate into titles? We'll be watching.

VICTOR OLADIPO 4

SOMETIMES A LITTLE swag goes a long way. We get that with Indiana Pacers star guard Victor Oladipo, who's added that extra spicy sauce to his game to elevate himself to one of the elite players at his position. It wasn't always this way, and Oladipo's rise to stardom has been hard work. Knowing him, he's not done yet; but for once, we should all acknowledge that he's finally arrived.

Born in the United States to African immigrants, Oladipo played high school ball in Hyattsville, Maryland, leading his team to a 32-4 record and scoring 11.9 points per game. He accepted a scholarship to play for Indiana University, one of basketball's meccas. Then-Indiana coach Tom Crean had also coached Dwyane Wade, a surefire future Hall of Famer. Crean saw a similar skill set in Oladipo — size, athleticism and a humble but confident attitude.

Rather than go one-and-done, the hardworking shooting guard honed his craft in college for three seasons. The Hoosiers made it to the Sweet Sixteen in his sophomore season, but Oladipo saved his best year for last. Oladipo was one of basketball's best college players, helping elevate his team to number one in the east. *Sporting News* named him Player of the Year, he was named the NABC Defensive Player of the Year (a title he shared), and NBA teams started targeting the best two-way guard in the country.

At 6-foot-4 and 210 pounds, he's a perfect blend of lightning-quick speed and raw athleticism. Add a killer shot and you have a perfect potion for success. That's what the Orlando Magic saw in him when they drafted him second overall in 2013. The Cleveland Cavaliers must be kicking themselves for passing on Oladipo because his college years were no fluke.

He recorded a triple-double just months into his rookie season. He played 80 games, starting 44, and averaged 13.8 points and 1.6 steals per contest. He played in the Rising Stars Challenge at the All-Star Game and finished second in Rookie of the Year voting to Michael Carter-Williams.

CAREER HIGHLIGHTS

- Named NBA Most Improved Player for 2017–18
- Named to NBA All-Rookie First Team in 2013–14
- Named to NBA All-Defensive First Team in 2017–18
- Has played in two All-Star Games (2018, 2019)
- Led the NBA in steals (177) in 2017–18

In his second year, Oladipo might be best remembered for the mask he wore after fracturing one of his facial bones in practice before the season started. His 2015 Slam Dunk Contest entrance was equally memorable, as the second-year player came out dressed to the nines. He put up a 540-windmill dunk, but it wasn't enough to beat Zach LaVine. He stuffed the stat sheet with 38 points following his debut at the dunk contest, and 30-point affairs became the regular. It felt like he'd be a Magic player for life, but in the summer of 2016, Oladipo was traded on draft night to the Oklahoma City Thunder for now-Toronto Raptors forward Serge Ibaka.

He played only one season for the Thunder before moving to Indiana alongside Domantis Sabonis (who also came to Oklahoma from Orlando) for Paul George. Oladipo had landed back where it all started — Indiana. He texted Domantis, "I promise, if you win here in Indiana, they'll embrace you like no other." He also said it was like "coming home."

That first season in Indiana, 2017–18, Oladipo was named Most Improved Player, made the All-Star Game as a reserve and led the Pacers into the playoffs. They pushed the Cavaliers to seven games thanks to Oladipo's triple-double in Game 6 — 28 points, 13 rebounds and 10 assists. He led the league in steals and headlined the NBA's All-Defensive Team. He posted the highest scoring numbers of his career (23.1 points, 2.4 steals per game) and

career-high numbers in free-throw percentage and three-point percentage.

The 2018–19 season started off much the same. The Pacers were plucky contenders in the east, and Oladipo was their main man. He was named an All-Star just as he suffered a season-ending quad injury. (The team still made the playoffs despite his absence but were cleanly swept by the Boston Celtics in the first round.)

Oladipo finds many sources of strength. He draws inspiration from his twin sister, who is deaf. He draws motivation because

of being traded twice, or "overlooked," as Oladipo calls it. These things make him work harder. He finished 2018–19 averaging 18.8 points per game, 5.6 rebounds and 5.2 assists.

The future is bright in Indiana. Oladipo is a bona fide star now, and that's what the Pacers need to compete in the east. He's already shown he can play clutch playoff ball. He's already shown he can lock down on defense, score at will and dunk on the main stage. At 27, he's now entering his prime. Buckle up for a ride.

BEN SIMMONS

BEN SIMMONS WAS a star even before he was drafted first overall in 2016. His journey to the NBA has been an unconventional one — the point guard hails from Australia, and only a handful of NBAers have made the leap from Down Under (current Golden State Warriors center Andrew Bogut is one of them). Since recovering from a foot injury that Simmons suffered in his first NBA preseason, which sidelined him for all of 2016–17, he's been making a massive impact plying his trade for the ever-improving Philadelphia 76ers — a team that's finally turned the corner from basement dweller to playoff contender. Simmons' play going forward will determine the fortunes of the new-look Sixers.

A high school stud in the city of Melbourne before moving to the United States in his sophomore year, Simmons had basketball pedigree written all over him thanks to an American father who once played in the NBA. The young point guard spent one year at Louisiana State University, amassing serious numbers across all categories. Simmons averaged 19.2 points per game over 33 contests, adding 11.8 rebounds and 4.8 assists for good measure.

After a disappointing season that saw LSU miss the NCAA tournament, Simmons set his sights on the NBA. The hype was huge. He even made an appearance on *The Tonight Show* with Jimmy Fallon prior to the 2016 NBA Draft, and everything seemed to be trending up. That is, until the injury. He

didn't make his NBA debut until October 2017. No matter — as the 76ers were rebuilding their franchise, patience was the order of the day. With center Joel Embiid, a beast in the middle, back to full health in 2016, Philly should be a lock for years to come with these two cornerstone pieces.

Simmons brings to the table a polished passing game and a creative scoring touch that's difficult to defend. His style causes fits for opposing coaches trying to match up against his athleticism. When Simmons is on the point, he's up against much smaller players. When he switches to the block, he's

too deft for big men to match his finesse. The last guard that tall running the point was a guy by the name of Magic Johnson, the Lakers Hall of Famer who changed the position. Simmons turned 23 years old in 2019, so the fluid guard/forward has plenty of time to figure out his fit within the system. One wonders if he may change the game.

Simmons put up a triple-double in just the second game of his rookie season (2017–18). But early January 2018 may have been Simmons at his finest. In 37 minutes against the Knicks, he scored 22 points, hauled down 22 boards and assisted on nine buckets. It wasn't quite a triple-double, but big numbers like this are the norm and double-digit assists regular occurrences. But don't expect Simmons to post 40-plus like some of the superstars in the league — he's more of a hybrid player, dishing and running the floor with the speed of a gazelle. That's what makes him so interesting. His court vision is off the charts, and his ability to dish is better than the back-of-house staff at a restaurant. Questions arise with his post-up game and jump shot, and both will need work for Simmons to become an elite player.

Cue 2018 and the fiasco in Minnesota that sent disgruntled guard Jimmy Butler to the Sixers for a few vets and a 2022 second-round draft pick. Butler immediately brought a grizzled, competitive attitude to the squad, something Simmons could use to light his own fire. Butler's experience added a whole new element in Philadelphia, a fanbase that loves no-nonsense athletes. The team spent the 2018–19 season yo-yoing in the middle of the playoff pack — midway through the campaign they were 30-16 — and the playoffs became a distinct reality for fans who suffered through the leanest of years. The exit of LeBron in the Eastern Conference opened up a lane for middle-of-the-pack teams to make a move, and the team locked up third place for the second straight season. Philly went to the second

round in the playoffs. Simmons, for his part, had a monster Game 6 to keep the series versus the Toronto Raptors alive, but the Sixers fell short in Game 7 after Kawhi Leonard's buzzer-beating series ender.

Will the 6-foot-10 guard from Australia be the answer after years of discontent in Philly? Only time will tell if Simmons is a once-in-a-generation player who, alongside Embiid and newly acquired Al Horford, can help deliver another championship to the City of Brotherly Love. In the meantime, grab a cheesesteak and pull up a seat.

CAREER HIGHLIGHTS

- Named NBA Rookie of the Year for 2017–18
- Named to NBA All-Rookie First Team in 2017–18
- Played in the 2019 NBA All-Star Game
- Named Rookie of the Month four times in 2017–18
- Named to the NCAA Men's Basketball All-American First Team in 2016

JAYSON TATUM 0

EVERY SO OFTEN, a player comes along and you just know he has it. Like, *it*. The "it factor," that special sauce, that extra somethin' somethin' that makes a player go from good to great. The Boston Celtics saw that in Jayson Tatum and made him their first-round selection in the 2017 NBA Draft. Since that fateful day, he's turned into one of the NBA's most promising rising stars, and the future looks bright in Boston.

At 6-foot-8 and 208 pounds, Tatum may look razor thin, but his skills are super sharp. His high school career was one to remember. He regularly posted 40-point games, leading his team to the Missouri state championship. He was named a McDonald's All-American and the Gatorade National Player of the Year in 2016. College teams came a-knockin', but Tatum inevitably chose Duke.

He didn't last long in college: the highly touted prospect jumped to the NBA after just one season. He was selected behind a couple of other rising stars, Markelle Fultz and Lonzo Ball. Philadelphia and Los Angeles may be regretting their decisions though, because Tatum has emerged as one of the best young players in the NBA and certainly the best of the first three draft picks in the 2017 class.

In his rookie season, Tatum posted 13.9 points per game while shooting 43 percent from three-point land and 83 percent from the stripe. In 80 games, all of which he started, he averaged 30 minutes per contest

— somewhat unheard of for a rookie. It just means Tatum is ready to become a major force in the league. This was most apparent during the Celtics' playoff run in 2018,

when Tatum helped lift his team to Game 7 of the Eastern Conference finals. He set several rookie playoff point records, but it wasn't enough. The Celtics eventually lost

CAREER HIGHLIGHTS

- Named to NBA All-Rookie First Team in 2017–18
- Won the All-Star Game Skills Challenge in 2019
- Played in the Rising Stars Challenge twice (2018, 2019)
- Finished eighth in three-point field goal percentage (.434) in 2017–18
- Named Rookie of the Month for December 2017

driving force of the Celtics' offense. Halfway through the season, he told Yahoo Sports, "I know I'm going to be an All-Star." It's that confidence that makes the difference between good and great, the it factor that has everyone wowing over the small forward with the sweet shot. It also meant Tatum was the subject of trade talks during the season when superstar Anthony Davis announced his intentions to leave New Orleans. Every team in the NBA wants a guy like Tatum — a young breakout star still on his rookie contract with a skill set that includes back-to-the-basket posts, fluid wing play and clutch shooting. He put up 34 against the Brooklyn Nets in January, and the following month, he started posting regular double-doubles. He's not a pass-first guy, so his assist numbers will never pop, but watch for his other stats to make heads turn.

He managed to turn heads at the 2019 All-Star Game when he played in the Rising Stars Challenge, scoring 30 points, and hit a half-court shot in the Skills Challenge that left tongues wagging in the stands. Suffice it to say, he's ready for the big stage, and there's no bigger one than playing in Boston night in, night out. Despite Tatum's flashes of brilliance in the 2019 playoffs — 26 points in Game 2 versus Indiana in the first round, 20 points and 11 rebounds in Game 3 versus Milwaukee in round two — the Celtics fell short of expectations and were eliminated by the Bucks.

Tatum is an integral piece of the puzzle moving forward, and as time goes by, his numbers will increase. More important, his role is going to change. Soon he's destined to become the go-to guy in the Celtics' offense, the all-potent wing who can spot-up shoot, post up or simply drain buckets. He may not be as flashy as some other stars in the league, but that shouldn't matter. When you've got the it factor, when you're that smooth, you let your play on the court do the talking. And if he keeps it up, Tatum will be part of the conversation for years to come.

to the Cleveland Cavaliers and LeBron James, but everyone will likely remember the moment after the loss, when King James pulled Tatum in for a hug and a whisper, apparently anointing another prince-in-waiting. The crown has been passed, and everyone awaited Tatum's sophomore campaign.

His numbers in 2018–19 showed improvement on already gaudy rookie stats. He averaged nearly 16 points, 6 rebounds and 85 percent from the free-throw line. Alongside Kyrie Irving, Tatum became a

POSITION CENTER / **SHOOTS** RIGHT / **HEIGHT** 7'0" / **WEIGHT** 248 LB. / **DRAFTED** 2015, MINNESOTA TIMBERWOLVES, 1ST OVERALL

KARL-ANTHONY TOWNS 32

TO SAY KARL-ANTHONY Towns has arrived is sort of like saying the Earth is round. No rookie made more of an impact on the NBA in 2015–16. Now, after concluding four years of NBA service, the 7-foot center has already proven to Minnesota Timberwolves brass and players around the league that he is no flash in the pan.

His rookie numbers were nothing short of spectacular — 18.3 points, 10.5 rebounds, 2 assists and 1.7 blocks per game. Towns took home the hardware for Rookie of the Year, which meant the T-Wolves captured back-to-back rookie trophies, with teammate Andrew Wiggins winning the 2014–15 honor. The decorated rookies have since formed the cornerstones of the Timberwolves team.

Born in Piscataway, New Jersey, Towns has been a phenom since birth. Literally. He was featured on a television news broadcast as a newborn in 1995 because of his extreme size — 10 pounds and 25 inches long, bigger than every other baby photographed that day. His parents scraped away to buy him a hoop and build a court on their property, and by the time he reached high school age, he was a dominant force against older boys and near perfect academically. Yet all the attention never seemed to fluster the even-keeled but ultra-competitive center. Instead, he channeled his energy into becoming the best player he could.

At 16 years old, Towns suited up for the national team of the Dominican Republic (his mother's home country) and played under University of Kentucky's legendary John Calipari, forming a relationship that continued when Towns attended Kentucky. Standing then at 6-foot-10, he'd already won a high school state title in New Jersey. Towns continued raking against older players before finally declaring his intent to play ball in the storied Kentucky program. He flourished in his only college year, averaging 10.3 points per game in just 21 minutes a night and helping his team make it all the

CAREER HIGHLIGHTS

- Named NBA Rookie of the Year for 2015–16
- Named to NBA All-Rookie First Team in 2015–16
- Has played in two All-Star Games (2018, 2019)
- Won the All-Star Game Skills Challenge in 2016
- Named to All-NBA Third Team in 2017–18

miss practice, arriving early and staying late, talking to himself. Towns also calls on an imaginary friend named Karlito to fire himself up. "You can't teach the beast," Garnett said early in Towns' rookie season, referring to his energy level. "You can't go to the store and buy a six-pack of beast."

The arrival of Jimmy Butler helped launch Minnesota into eighth spot in 2017–18, but the team was quickly ousted in the playoffs by Houston. Towns' overall numbers dipped, and questions of chemistry among the group spilled into the off-season, culminating in an infamous pre-season practice in which Butler called out the young team and the Minnesota brass.

In 2018–19 Towns delivered on the stat sheet, but the T-Wolves fell short of the playoffs, and Towns' streak of 303 consecutive games as a starter ended after a car accident forced him to the sidelines for a couple of games in mid-February. The center still played 77 games and finished 13th in league scoring (24.4) and 7th in rebounding (12.4). Minnesota is Towns' team again — Butler was traded to Philadelphia in November 2018 — so the franchise's fortunes will largely fall on the shoulders of their star player.

A perfect blend of intelligence, ambition, talent and will, Towns has been given the tools by numerous mentors and handed the keys to the franchise. Now it's time for the young phenom to grow into the man. At 7 feet and 248 pounds, he's well on his way.

way to the Final Four. After entering the 2015 NBA Draft, he landed in Minnesota as their number one pick.

Towns has fast become one of the most complete big men on the hardcourt. He posts up, steps back, spins, runs the court, plays D — the list goes on. The crazy thing? He improved in nearly every offensive category in 2016–17 and nearly held up his impressive averages in the subsequent seasons. Plus he's capable of making opponents look silly anytime, anywhere. Take the 41 points and 16 rebounds he put up versus Houston just before Christmas

2016, the franchise record 56 points he put up in March 2018 or the last three games of February 2019 when he averaged nearly 38 points and 19 rebounds a game. He's an automatic double-double every night and someone who can carry the Wolves when the guards go cold.

More important, his willingness to learn and get better is off the charts. He lapped up every drop of knowledge mentor and retired veteran Kevin Garnett offered. "The best thing to ever happen to Karl is Garnett," Towns' father once said. Garnett displayed legendary intensity, refusing to

POSITION SMALL FORWARD / **SHOOTS** RIGHT / **HEIGHT** 6'8" / **WEIGHT** 194 LB. / **DRAFTED** 2014, CLEVELAND CAVALIERS, 1ST OVERALL

ANDREW WIGGINS 22

NOT MANY NBA rookies have had to deal with as much fame as Canadian Andrew Wiggins. The first overall pick of the 2014 draft has handled the circus with aplomb and grace, qualities sure to be fundamental as he embarks on a long career in the NBA.

Hailing from Toronto, Ontario, the new hotbed of international basketball, Wiggins was a rising star as a teenager and was quickly noticed by pundits down south. Like other Canadians before him, he chose to play for the prestigious Huntington Prep High School in West Virginia, an incubator for future NBA talent.

Wiggins then shipped off to the University of Kansas for a classic one-and-done experience. All freshman year, Wiggins, under the tutelage of coach Bill Self, was the talk of the NCAA. In 35 games with the Jayhawks, Wiggins averaged a team-high 17.1 points per game, as well as 5.9 rebounds and 1.5 assists. Although the numbers weren't eye-popping, the fact Wiggins had just turned 19 fueled speculations he'd go first or second overall. Possessing raw athleticism, smooth jumping ability, sound defensive awareness and an otherworldly vertical of 44 inches (among the highest ever recorded), Wiggins was drafted by the Cleveland Cavaliers first overall. It appeared he would play student under the mentorship of LeBron James; however, rumors abounded the Cavs were looking for another piece to their push for a championship — the Minnesota

Timberwolves' Kevin Love. Wiggins, meanwhile, had signed with the Cavs and could not be traded for a 30-day period owing to a clause in the collective bargaining

agreement. Thus, the 19-year-old remained in limbo until the deal could be formalized. In August 2014, Wiggins became the second number one draft pick since 1976 to never

CAREER HIGHLIGHTS

- Named NBA Rookie of the Year for 2014–15
- Named to NBA All-Rookie First Team in 2014–15
- Named Rookie of the Month four times in 2014–15
- Is only the second Canadian to be selected first overall in the NBA draft
- Named Gatorade National Player of the Year in 2013

play for the team that drafted him when Cleveland sent Wiggins to Minnesota for Kevin Love.

When the T-Wolves finally introduced Wiggins to the public, he was all smiles. "It's been a crazy summer," he said. "But I wanted to play for a team that wanted me." Minneapolis is the chilliest city in the NBA, so the Canadian should feel right at home. As Wiggins told Bill Self at the time, "It's better for me . . . to go somewhere where I'm forced to be something."

His first game for Minnesota was largely forgettable (6 points in 19 minutes of play), but he improved throughout the year, recording his first double-double in early December (23 points and 10 assists) in an upset win over the Portland Trail Blazers. On his 20th birthday in late February 2015, he scored 30 points, proving he possesses the panache to be dominant in the league. Wiggins became the first Timberwolves player to win Rookie of the Year, finishing with 16.9 points and 4.6 rebounds per game.

Despite a losing season in his first year with Minnesota, Wiggins proved he could be a go-to option from the perimeter and a basket-attacking force of nature. In his second year, he registered 32 points, 10 boards and 6 assists against the Sacramento Kings in December, joining an elite company — with members like LeBron James and Kevin Durant — of 20-and-under superstars who can put up that kind of stat line. In 2016–17, he averaged 23.6 points a

night while playing over 37 minutes a game. He showed flashes of brilliance throughout the season, including a career-high 47-point night in November versus the LA Lakers and back-to-back 40-point affairs late in the season.

Wiggins' 2017–18 and 2018–19 seasons can be looked at in several ways. On one hand, they could be considered another growing experience for the young star. On the other, so much is expected of the former Rookie of the Year, who now has five seasons under his belt and has shown only incremental degrees of improvement. Although he did score 40 against the Oklahoma City Thunder midway through 2018–19, he barely cracked the top 40 in scoring that season. His 18.1 points over

35 minutes a night is a far cry from the nearly 24 a game he poured in during his 2016–17 campaign. The Timberwolves were eliminated quickly in the 2018 playoffs and missed the 2019 playoffs altogether, and since then a number of "what ifs" have surfaced.

The talent for the young Canadian is undoubtedly there — it's simply a matter of his taking the next step in his career. He's signed to a five-year, $148 million contract through 2022–23, so expectations are high. Will Wiggins and teammate Karl-Anthony Towns, another first overall pick, rise to the occasion and transform Minnesota into a dominant presence? Only time will tell, but this dynamic duo will certainly be the pair to watch.

THE PLAYOFFS

THE REGULAR SEASON is like a warm-up jacket or a practice jersey, an opening act if you will. Most of the work is done in the lengthy grind, and it does separate the real athletes from the pretenders, but postseason performances are where careers are forged and reputations made. Regardless of regular-season numbers or record-setting seasons, it's rings that matter, not points per game. Whether that's fair or not is another conversation entirely. But in basketball, what separates the good from the great is your ability to come through when it truly matters.

Like the clutch performance conversation, the debate never ceases to double-back on the same questions. Who was the greatest of all time when it mattered most? Who stepped up at a crucial moment? Immortality and everlasting fame, in the annals of sport, art and war, have always been more interesting than one brief moment of glory. Since the days of gladiator pits, the Trojan War and the sacking of cities, having one's name written down in the record books is what lifts men from mere mortals to gods. Modern times are no different, and in the sport of basketball, the playoffs are king. So what better way to start than with the reigning monarch of the court?

The Cleveland Cavaliers' LeBron James answers questions at a press conference following Game 7 of the 2016 NBA Finals. The Cavs defeated the Golden State Warriors to claim Cleveland's first-ever NBA championship.

KING JAMES VERSUS MICHAEL JORDAN

LeBron James — LeBron — the single-name, one-man highlight reel, has succeeded so thoroughly that fans don't even notice how easy he makes it look. A lightning rod for praise and criticism, James appeared in eight straight finals from 2011 to 2018, the first to do so since Bill Russell made 10 straight from 1957 to 1966. He's won the regular-season MVP award four times, so we know how good a player he is on the march to glory. But what about the finish? With three wins and six losses in nine trips, he's been, well, middle of the road with respect to those rings. And of course, it wasn't without controversy that he and Chris Bosh flipped the tables on free agency and agreed to sign with the Miami Heat to join friend and All-Star Dwyane Wade. Manufactured? Sure. But that doesn't dismiss the fact that LeBron led the Heat through four straight seasons and four straight postseasons. That's a lot of wear and tear and playing consistently at a high level, so no wonder he was banged up early in 2014. But as he continues through his mid-thirties, the discussion has focused less on his choices and more on his legacy, specifically related to Michael Jordan.

LeBron will always be compared with Jordan, no matter how well or poorly he does. An ESPN poll in 2015 said 34 percent of people think Jordan, who was 52 years of age at the time, could beat a then-30-year-old James in a game of 1-on-1. That's how wonky and clickbait-driven the debate can get. Perhaps one-third of the public might need to be reminded that LeBron continues to bust up Jordan's numbers.

In the third round of the 2014–15 playoffs against the Atlanta Hawks, James eclipsed Jordan's record of 51 games with at least 30 points, 5 rebounds and 5 assists. Kobe, the next closest, had a mere 37 to his name and played in 220 playoff games in his career, as compared to LeBron's 239 games as of 2019, the first year he's missed the playoffs in a decade. In Game 3 of the 2014–15 Atlanta series, with both Kevin Love and Kyrie Irving injured, James scored 38 points, pulled 18 off the glass and dished out 13 assists for the triple-double, all the while hobbled by injuries to his ankle and back and suffering from cramping. And he started the game 0 for 10 from the field! No player has ever posted a line like that, regular season or postseason. The closest? Charles Barkley back in 1993, who stuck 43 points, 15 boards and 10 dimes in Game 5 of the Western Conference

Michael Jordan cradles the NBA championship trophy in 1993 following the Chicago Bulls' 99–98 win over the Phoenix Suns for their third straight title.

finals. LeBron passed Kareem Abdul-Jabbar and Jerry West for 30-plus-point playoff games, then in the 2018 NBA Finals versus the Warriors, he passed Jordan for first all-time. He also sits second behind Magic Johnson for most triple-doubles in the postseason, who it should be mentioned, feels more comparable than Jordan ever will be.

Despite all this, LeBron's had to somehow work harder to outlive the legacy of Jordan. It's likely very simple: MJ never lost in the finals, going 6-0. LeBron, just by losing in the NBA Finals, draws the ire of purists. In 2015, James almost equaled Jordan's 1993 record for highest percentage of his team's points, 38.4 percent to 38.3. However, he long ago shattered Jordan's best PER of 32.04 with a

mark of 37.39 (2009), which is second all-time to Jordan's draft mate, Hakeem Olajuwon (38.96).

When James launched himself up from the corner in the dying seconds of Game 4 of the 2015 Eastern Conference semifinals versus the Chicago Bulls, it was just the third playoff buzzer beater of his career at that point, which many were quick to point out is in fact the same number Michael Jordan has, and yet His Airness' buzzer beaters are somehow legend. James' first: Game 2 of the 2008–09 Eastern Conference finals against the Orlando Magic. With one second on the clock he drained a shot from three-point land to secure victory. James and the Cavaliers eventually lost that series, but LeBron did just about everything over the course of six games: 38.5 points, 8.3 rebounds, 8.3 assists, 49 percent from the field, all in 44.3 minutes a game. That is some next-level business, but the performance is largely forgotten, as is his PER from that entire playoffs.

Conversely, what isn't soon to fade from memory is Jordan's series-ender versus Cleveland in 1989, a touchstone moment in his career. His finals-finisher a decade later in 1998 was just as great, when in Game 6, he sealed the deal on the Bulls' sixth and last ring with a 20-foot jumper with five seconds left. It wasn't technically a buzzer beater, but considering the circumstances, it was just as big. Plus, what's likely forgotten about that 1998 final is that in the 87–86 Game 6 win, Jordan scored a crucial bucket with a minute to go and then stole the ball from Karl Malone to set up the final points. It would be his last title, and probably the lasting image of a great career despite several comebacks and retirements.

For James, many may remember the 2014–15 NBA Finals, not for the Golden State Warriors' win, but for the He-Man-like performance of James. It wasn't a one-shot performance for the King; instead it will quite possibly go down as the definition of a one-man team — LeBron versus the Warriors. After losing his fellow star teammates Love and Irving to injury, James lugged Cleveland's bench players on his back as he battled his way game after game. He played 275 minutes out of a possible 298 and averaged 38 points, 13.3 rebounds and 8.8 assists. A horde of voices called for LeBron to be named the MVP despite the series loss. It would have made him the first player to be so named since "Mr. Clutch" Jerry West in 1969. James received four of 11 votes, but it wasn't enough to take the award from the hands of the man who won it — Andre Iguodala, who was picked for his work guarding the Cleveland star. Even with the Warriors' small forward pestering him, James became the first player in the history of the NBA Finals to lead both teams in points, rebounds and assists. That is plain ridiculous.

The following season he avenged his 2015 finals loss, capturing his third title and finally etching himself in lore — not with a clutch shot but with a clutch play now known as "the Block." Running full-speed down the court, he caught up to Iguodala, the man who took his MVP award the year before, and swatted away a potential game-winning basket in the final minutes.

Despite James' three rings to Jordan's six, LeBron's done the work to be called the best ever.

The injured Willis Reed, right, battles with Wilt Chamberlain in Game 7 of the 1970 NBA Finals. Reed's perseverance through injury to help his Knicks win the title was instantly made legend.

OVERCOMING ADVERSITY

Greatness and adversity. Combine the two and you get the stuff of legends. When Isiah Thomas scored 43 points, 25 in one quarter, and added 8 assists and 6 steals in the 1988 NBA Finals while hobbling around on one ankle for the Detroit Pistons, it established a modern-day tale of playing through injury.

The performance was a throwback to what many call the gutsiest comeback in NBA history. That belongs to Willis Reed, the hulking 6-foot-9, 235-pound center of the 1969–70 New York Knicks. It was LA versus New York in a hotly contested NBA championship that came down to the final game. Reed, who had badly injured his right leg in Game 5 after trying to elude the also-ailing Wilt Chamberlain, missed Game 6, and the Lakers forced the pivotal seventh game back in New York at the fabled Madison Square Garden.

Teammates had implored the injured Reed to give them 20 minutes. But as the warm-ups started, Reed was still in the trainer's room.

"I wanted to play," Reed recalled when recounting the story to NBA.com. "That was the championship . . . I didn't want to have to look at myself in the mirror 20 years later and say that I wished I had tried to play."

Reed also remembers that the needle used for the painkillers was huge, and just the act of administering the medicine caused him a lot of pain.

But as he limped to the floor the Garden fans rose up; the players stopped warm-ups, and a tidal wave of appreciative support rained down on Reed and the Knicks.

Dallas Mavericks forward Dirk Nowitzki shoots against the Oklahoma City Thunder during the 2011 Western Conference finals. Nowitzki and Dallas went on to win the NBA title that year.

He didn't throw down many points or hit a buzzer beater. But he was serviceable, keeping Chamberlain to 10 field goals and 2 for 9 in the paint. More telling was the emotional lift it gave his teammates, who ably picked up their center, winning 113–99. It was the Knicks' first-ever title.

Not surprisingly, Michael Jordan added his own power-through-adversity game to the list of the NBA's greatest moments when in 1998 he played in what is known today as "the Flu Game."

The contest is a well-established chronicle — a standout moment from his laundry list of impressive feats.

To recap: It's Game 5 of the NBA Finals and Jordan, who woke up nauseated, dehydrated and fatigued, missed morning practice but donned the jersey come game time. Clearly not himself, Jordan started off slowly but eventually willed himself to drop 30 on the Jazz. With the Bulls victorious, Jordan fell into Scottie Pippen's arms at the end of the game, an enduring image of his exhaustion. They would finish off Utah in Game 6, the sixth and final championship Jordan and the Bulls won. Jordan was named MVP after depositing 39 points to seal the deal. Many thought it was a typical flu, but in 2013, Jordan's former personal trainer would tell the real truth: it was in fact food poisoning the night before the game. A legend was born from a bad pizza ordered late at night in Salt Lake City that did His Airness in. "That was probably the most difficult thing I've ever done," Jordan would say to NBA.com about the night that became

established in NBA lore. It goes down as one of the greatest playoff performances in the history of the NBA.

BUT OVERCOMING ADVERSITY isn't just prevailing when you are physically down and out. It can be stepping up in critical ways when the odds are stacked against you.

On May 13, 2004, not one but two incredible shots occurred back to back in the Western Conference semifinals. After dropping the first two games of the series against the San Antonio Spurs, the LA Lakers stormed back, capped off by their improbable 74–73 Game 5 victory on the road. Derek Fisher's dagger with 0.4 seconds left dispatched the Spurs that evening, and the fact he even got it off with nearly no time remaining was mind-blowing. The fact he actually sunk it established Fisher's rep as a money-ball shooter who rose to the big occasion.

To add to the legend, the unbelievable shot came directly after Tim Duncan hit his own improbable, off-balance 18-footer from the top of the key with Shaquille O'Neal in his face to go ahead by one point. Rare the day it's been when two dying-second shots happen in near synchronicity, and the image of Fisher — running off the court and into the tunnel with a trail of teammates following — is lodged in the collective memory bank of NBA fans.

Dirk Nowitzki, too, had to overcome adversity to earn the respect he rightfully deserved.

Bill Russell loops a hook shot over the head of Jim Krebs of the Los Angeles Lakers in the 1962 NBA Finals. Russell and his Boston Celtics took the series in seven games.

Anyone in the league would let you know that the German is a damn good ball player, but his 48-point performance in the 2011 Western Conference finals versus Oklahoma cemented a long, impressive career. Critics loved to pick apart the mostly hollow theory that the Euro was a choker.

In 2006, the Mavericks made the NBA Finals for the first time in his tenure but lost the championship to the Dwyane Wade–led Miami Heat after leading 2-0. People forget Dirk went off for 50 that year in the Western Conference finals versus Phoenix, scoring 22 in the final frame of Game 5. The following season, the Mavericks lost in the first round to eighth seed Golden State — the same year Nowitzki won MVP — the first time a number one seed lost to an eighth. Despite being the most dominant player in the league, with an NBA Finals trip and an MVP nod, it seemed an asterisk always followed Nowitzki.

Until 2011.

Finally given the chance to expunge his critics, the floppy-haired German hoisted a now underdog Mavs team on his back in Game 1 of the 2011 Western Conference finals against the surging Oklahoma Thunder, who boasted Durant, Westbrook and Harden. Dirk sent a message with 48 points on 12-of-15 shooting, including an astronomical 24 of 24 from the line. He missed just three shots the entire night. Dallas silenced Oklahoma over the course of the series, and Nowitzki exacted revenge on the Heat in a rematch of the 2006 finals, defeating another sparkling trio of James, Wade and Bosh. He finally shed the image of a playoff choker and was named NBA Finals MVP. That 48-point night where he barely missed a basket set the tone, and the rest is history.

BIGS PLAYING BIG

Big moments from physically large men. For years, that was almost exclusively what the NBA offered.

Before the widening of the key and the establishment of the three-point line, bigs ruled the roost — sitting under the bucket in the paint, depositing pick-and-roll plays or scooping up errant outside jumpers for putbacks. Players like George Mikan, Bill Walton and Kareem Abdul-Jabbar etched legendary postseason performances. Then, in another stratosphere, is Bill Russell.

Most of us probably don't remember the 1962 NBA Finals, but it featured the two storied franchises in the NBA at the time: the Boston Celtics and Los Angeles Lakers. It pitted east versus west and is the last NBA Finals Game 7 to ever go to overtime. Inside the eventual Celtics series win were two monumental performances. Lakers forward Elgin Baylor put up 61 points (and 22 boards) in Game 5 on the road, a finals record that remains today. (Jordan holds the all-time single-game playoff record with 63 points in 1986, the first glimpse into his superstardom.) Baylor's 33 points in one half stood for 25 years until Eric "Sleepy" Floyd broke the record in 1987 (more on that later). In Game 7, though, the tables turned.

Hakeem Olajuwon climbs the ladder over San Antonio Spurs forward Dennis Rodman for one of his 75 rebounds over the course of the series.

Bill Russell dominated the game, putting up 30 points and an astronomical mark of 40 rebounds. Russell collected 370 total rebounds in 14 playoff games that season — and in his career that is only his third best playoff showing. His averages of 22.9 points, 27 rebounds, and 5.7 assists sealed the deal for the Celtics, who would go on to win several more rings that decade during their dynasty run. Russell finished his playoff career 10-0 in Game 7s, which says a little something about rising to the occasion.

The Lakers also figured in on many great playoff performances, and one was during the 2000 NBA Finals from the man who was as big as they came. Shaq.

At 7-foot-1 and 325 pounds, the Big Aristotle could dominate, but there's a difference between utter dominance and a quiet, controlled supremacy.

When the Lakers beat the Pacers in the 2000 NBA Finals, Shaquille O'Neal posted a not-so-subtle line of 43 points and 19 rebounds in Game 1. It set the tone for a dominant series that saw O'Neal emerge as the go-to man after 21-year-old Kobe Bryant suffered an ankle injury midway through the series when Jalen Rose stepped on said joint. Shaq finished with no fewer than 33 points in any game, and in Game 6, he dropped 41 points and 12 rebounds against a guard-heavy Pacers team that starred Reggie Miller. O'Neal dominated an aging 7-foot-4 Rik Smits in the paint, and with the Pacers hacking Shaq at every opportunity thanks to his poor free-throwing skills, he made enough from the stripe to seal the win.

Although he may lack the rings of Shaq, Bryant or Jordan, Hakeem Olajuwon took his Houston Rockets to two titles and posted massive playoff numbers during his career that largely go unnoticed.

In 1987, Hakeem the Dream posted a 49-point, 25-rebound, 6-block night, years before he'd win those back-to-back titles in the mid-90s. In 1988, although Houston was swept by the Dallas Mavericks, it wasn't due to a lack of effort from Olajuwon. The Houston big averaged 37.5 points and 16.8 rebounds per game.

And what about those back-to-back titles? The Dream put up averages of 28.9 points and 11 rebounds in 1994, and 33 and 10.3 in 1995.

The 1995 Western Conference finals was the stuff of legend for Olajuwon. Facing off against David Robinson, Dennis Rodman and the San Antonio Spurs, the Houston center dominated, putting up 40-plus points in three of the series' six games, and 39 in the final contest. Robinson cracked 30 only once against Houston, and needing a win in Game 6 to stay alive, he mustered only 19 points.

Olajuwon's record-setting PER was set during the lost playoff opportunity against Dallas in 1987, but he kept on working and was eventually rewarded.

The late great Wilt Chamberlain owns a laundry list of NBA play-off records, including most rebounds in one postseason game (41), despite winning the ultimate prize only twice in his career. The man has his own Wikipedia page just for records he's set. If the argument of greatest playoff performers is based solely on titles, however, Wilt's not even in the conversation.

But there's no doubt he was one of the most dominant postseason performers of his era. He led the NBA in playoff rebounds per game in eight of the 13 seasons his teams made the extra session. And in the five seasons he didn't lead the league, he was second.

Even late in his career, working under the rim for the LA Lakers, Chamberlain was effective. He was able to leave the scoring to

others, and at 35 on the 1972 Lakers title winners, he averaged a double-double and led the league in rebounds.

THE GREATEST PLAYOFF PERFORMER YOU'VE NEVER HEARD OF

One man dared take on the mighty LA Lakers in the 1987 playoffs. Before the Bulls made their legendary run in the 90s, there was the Magic Johnson–led Lakers, the crème de la crème of the NBA a decade prior to Jordan's reign. Kareem Abdul-Jabbar and James Worthy rounded out an All-Star cast of characters that would lift the trophy that season, their fourth since 1980. The Golden State Warriors had missed the dance for years but surprisingly sent the Utah Jazz home in the first round after staging an improbable comeback after being down 2-0. They won the clinching Game 5 on the road in Salt Lake City. Their second-round prize? A group of goliaths who had already drunk champagne in 1980, 1982 and 1985. But in 1987, one man dared take on those mighty Lakers. Entering Game 4, Golden State had lost three straight, and by a hefty margin. But that night, the Warriors woke up. Or one man did. His name was Sleepy Floyd.

Eric "Sleepy" Floyd averaged just 12.8 points per game over his admirable 14-year career, but one evening stands above the rest. The 1986–87 season was perhaps his most complete — he made the All-Star Game and averaged 18.8 points and 10.3 assists. But down 3-0 that postseason to the Lakers, Sleepy'd had enough. By the time the game finished, Floyd had single-handedly taken down the best squad of NBA players in the league. At one point, he made 12 field goals in a row. One writer said following the game: "The hair on my neck was standing. The most incredible feeling I've ever had at a sporting event." The YouTube clip of the highlights is equally goosebump-inducing.

The former Georgetown star finished the game with 51 points, etching himself in the basketball history books with an unimaginable, out-of-nowhere performance. The current Warriors team, with the likes of hot-handed Splash Brothers Steph Curry and Klay Thompson, almost feel like heir apparents to Sleepy's record since their dominance of the Western Conference starting in 2014–15 and their marches to the 2015, 2017 and 2018 NBA titles. Thompson especially: in 2014–15, he set the regular-season record for most points in a quarter, dropping an en fuego 37 points in the third quarter versus Sacramento midway through the season, finishing 13 of 13 with 9 three-pointers. Perhaps Thompson channeled that epic night of Sleepy Floyd, as now both the regular-season and playoff record for most points in a quarter belong to members of Golden State.

Further, that year Curry set the playoff record for most threes made, and he did it by the second quarter of Game 3 of the Western Conference finals, eclipsing Reggie Miller's mark of 58. Curry and the Warriors still had five wins to go to claim the championship, and in the two quarters and eight games after he set the mark and the Warriors collected their five wins, Curry added 39 more threes. His new mark of 98 seems assailable by only Thompson (who tied it in 2016) and himself.

Eric Floyd drives to the basket during the fourth quarter of his record-setting 51-point playoff game against the Los Angeles Lakers in 1987.

ALTHOUGH CHAMPIONSHIP RINGS may be a starting and end point for some fans, what should make the most difference is how a player affected the outcome of a game or a series. Not one player can do it all and will a team to a championship — the Charles Barkleys and Reggie Millers of the world will always walk around with naked fingers and broken dreams. LeBron couldn't haul a 2007 Cleveland team on his back, and try as he might in 2015, he couldn't do it then, either. (Although he avenged the 2015 loss the next season, he still needed Kyrie Irving's last-minute heroics to get there.) With his career now in the rearview mirror, LeBron's a perfect example of someone with a brilliant yet flawed NBA Finals record of 3-6. He's won, he's lost, and he's dominated at every step of the way. No one should doubt the man's ability to rise to the occasion. There are many different ways to measure success. Character and heart sometimes don't line up with numbers. On other nights, whether Michael's battling the flu or Isiah's fighting a twisted ankle, greatness occurs and enters into the lore of playoff basketball forever.

UNSUNG HEROES

C.J. McCOLLUM

BRADLEY BEAL [3]

IF EVER THERE was a basketball player who belonged in the Old West, it's Bradley Beal of the Washington Wizards. He's a gunslinger, a sharpshooter, a guard with swagger who has consistently proven he belongs among the elite class of NBA players.

It all began in St. Louis, Missouri. Beal's mom was a former Kentucky State standout and a high school coach, known as "Mama Lion" — something he told *The Players' Tribune* in 2017. Equipped with a hunger to be better, Beal endured all manner of trials and tribulations — including matching up against his two younger brothers, both 300-pound college linemen — to finish high school with a 3.9 GPA, the 2011 Gatorade Player of the Year award and a scholarship to the University of Florida. Beal learned the Xs and Os under famed coach Billy Donovan, and as a freshman in college, he averaged 14.8 points and 6.7 rebounds.

For nearly his entire career, Beal, a 6-foot-5, 207-pound shooting guard, has played second fiddle to another alpha dog in the nation's capital — point guard John Wall, the first overall pick in the 2010 draft. Beal was drafted two years later, third overall after only one season of college ball, during which he helped the Gators make the Elite Eight of the 2012 NCAA tournament.

The Wizards were a team in transition when Beal arrived, having missed the playoffs four consecutive seasons. Beal got injured just past the midway point of the

with a five-year, $127 million contract, he played 77 games, the most in his career up to that point. He set career highs in field goal percentage (.482) and free-throw percentage (.825). The Wizards soared, seemingly employing basketball sorcery along the way. The team finished first in the Southeast Division, fourth in the conference, and seemed poised to exorcise past postseason demons. Beal, for his part, was regularly posting 40-point games. The Wizards exacted revenge on the Hawks in six games, and the Boston Celtics lay in wait in the second round. Beal dropped 38 points in Game 7, but Washington eventually succumbed to the Celtics 115-105. Despite the heartbreaking loss, Beal's reputation as clutch had been cemented.

The 2018–19 season was a different story for the perennial playoff contenders. The Wizards were once again in chaos, and Wall exited stage left with a season-ending injury halfway through the campaign. This development suddenly thrust Beal into the spotlight — his team, his game, the ball in his hand, just like those days in St. Louis and Florida when he was the top dog. In January, in a double-overtime loss versus the Raptors, Beal recorded a triple-double — 43 points, 15 assists and 10 boards — showcasing his full skill set. In March he went back-to-back games with 40 points, hitting seven and nine threes, respectively, as he displayed his spot shooting and pushed for the postseason. Washington failed to sneak into the playoff picture — they fell just short in the competitive east — but Beal certainly proved his mettle. He averaged a career-high 25.6 points per game, good for top 15 in the NBA, and for a guy who's been injury prone, the shooting guard led the league in minutes played and was the only player in the upper echelon of NBA scorers to play all 82 games.

Beal's vaulted himself into All-Star status for the second straight year and has everyone asking the question, is he All-NBA? At just 26, the seasoned veteran is entering his prime with both seven seasons under his belt and miles to go. Just what is still in his holster remains to be seen.

CAREER HIGHLIGHTS

- Named to NBA All-Rookie First Team in 2012–13
- Has played in two All-Star Games (2018, 2019)
- Led the NBA in minutes played in 2018–19
- Is a two-time NBA Rookie of the Month
- Is a three-time NBA Player of the Week

year but came back healthy in his sophomore campaign, scoring a then-career-best 37 points against the Memphis Grizzlies and upping his points per game average from 14 in his first year to over 17 in his second. Beal and Wall took Washington into the postseason and won the first round for the first time in nearly a decade. The Wizards had their one-two punch — the flashy, pass-first speed demon in Wall and the lethal gunslinger in Beal.

Despite wrist and toe injuries in 2014–15, Beal helped lead the Wiz to a 46-36 record (good for fifth in the Eastern Conference), and they swept the Toronto Raptors in the first round. In the second round, a hobbling Beal was Washington's top scorer in five out of six games against the Atlanta Hawks, but playoff disappointment would strike again — a recurrent theme for the two stars, who struggle to get the team over the hump.

Beal enjoyed one of his best seasons, and a healthy one to boot, in 2016–17. Armed

POSITION POINT GUARD / **SHOOTS** LEFT / **HEIGHT** 6'1" / **WEIGHT** 175 LB. / **DRAFTED** 2007, MEMPHIS GRIZZLIES, 4TH OVERALL

MIKE CONLEY  10

AT 6-FOOT-1 AND 175 pounds, Mike Conley isn't the biggest point guard in the league. And despite his name being absent from conversations about the best players at the position, he helped lead the resurgent Memphis Grizzlies to levels never before seen by the franchise. Make no mistake: Mike Conley has slowly matured into one of the most consistent difference makers in the NBA today.

Conley comes from athletic pedigree — his father, Mike Conley Sr., won gold at the 1992 Olympics in triple jump, and his uncle played linebacker for the Pittsburgh Steelers. Mike starred at Ohio State as a point guard for one season for the Buckeyes alongside future number one pick Greg Oden. The duo led the school to the 2007 NCAA final, where they lost to a power-house Florida team. But before making the jump to Ohio and then the NBA, Oden and Conley were a force to be reckoned with, destroying the high school basketball scene in Indiana while amassing a 103-7 record with Lawrence North High School in Indianapolis. The duo led the Hoosier state to three state championships.

When Ohio State coach Thad Matta recruited the two stars together, he said that people laughed at him because he thought Conley was "the best point guard in the country," despite the fact that "he played with Greg." Matta, of course, is having the last laugh now (Oden was hampered by injuries and never amounted to the hype).

Conley, on the other hand, has been durable and effective, running the offense for the Grizz over the last 12 years. In 2018–19 he posted a career-high 21.1 points per game in addition to 6.4 assists. The court general has maintained a free-throw percentage of more than 80 percent and has shot 37.5 percent from behind the arc his entire NBA career. He may not lead the Grizzlies in any one category, but his presence on the court and what he means to his team aren't found on the score sheet.

It's been slow and steady progress, however. After being drafted fourth overall, he started just 46 games his rookie year. By year two, he clocked in at 60, but his numbers were average, and he was sharing time in an untenable situation with future All-Star Kyle Lowry, who'd been drafted one

Perhaps his most admirable, unquantifiable quality is his ability to get guys going. Conley is a whiz at noticing when his teammates need the ball — "it's almost like you have a clock in your head," he once said — or knowing when he needs to slash toward the hoop to give the team an energy boost. He helped take the team to the Western Conference finals in 2012, which is the farthest the franchise has gone in its history.

The 2014–15 playoffs were tough on the undersized guard. Already playing with a wonky ankle, he suffered a facial fracture that required surgery at the end of the Grizzlies' first-round victory over the Portland Trail Blazers. Conley gamely came back in the second round wearing a face mask versus the Golden State Warriors and sparked the Grizz to victory in Game 2 on the road. Conley's 22 points on 8-of-10 shooting underscore the emotional impact he brought to the arena that night, but it wasn't enough, and the Grizzlies' season ended at the hands of Golden State. In 2016–17, after re-signing with Memphis for a hefty $153 million over five years, Conley didn't simply sit on his newfound dough — he averaged 20.5 points and 3.5 rebounds per game and hit treys at a 40 percent clip. He led the Memphis squad back to the playoffs, only to fall to the San Antonio Spurs in six games.

Conley played only 12 games in 2017–18 because of injury, but he returned the following season with a vengeance. The Grizz got off to a great start in 2018–19, but they faltered midway through the season. The team begrudgingly started to sell off pieces: Memphis parted ways with long-time center Marc Gasol, trading the Spaniard to Toronto and leaving Conley to shoulder the load for the remainder of the season. Traded to the Utah Jazz a day before the 2019 draft, Conley will now take his talents to Salt Lake City, where he'll become a key playmaker on an up-and-coming Jazz squad.

Conley's been labeled both an underachiever and underrated, but it's about time both tags are shed in favor of what he actually is: a wily veteran who is one of the NBA's great court generals.

CAREER HIGHLIGHTS

- Won the NBA Sportsmanship Award two times (2013–14, 2018–19)
- Won the Twyman-Stokes Teammate of the Year Award in 2018–19
- Named to NBA All-Defensive Second Team in 2012–13
- Tied a career high in points (40) in 2018–19
- Set a career high in points per game (21.1) in 2018–19

year ahead of Conley. Lowry was eventually traded in 2009 to Houston, and Conley took over the Grizzlies' point guard position.

He plays primarily left-handed — despite actually being right-handed — but uses his right to drain his money shot, a short-range floater that he's been good for at more than 50 percent in recent years.

ANDRE DRUMMOND

YOU CAN'T IGNORE Andre Drummond. He's a beast in the Eastern Conference, yanking boards off the glass for the Detroit Pistons like a seasoned apple picker. At 26 years old, the center is just entering his prime years. The talent and size are there for him to become a superstar, and the 2018–19 season will go down as his breakout campaign.

Drummond suited up for the UConn Huskies in his first and only season in the NCAA as a walk-on, meaning he didn't have a scholarship. The team was fresh off a championship run thanks to the heroics of another future NBAer, Shabazz Napier, and the freshman center proved his immediate worth by leading the team in rebounds, blocks and field goal percentage. Considered one of the top prospects in the country, Drummond jumped at the chance to enter the NBA, going ninth overall to the Detroit Pistons in a draft that saw a bevy of future NBA talent, such as Anthony Davis, Bradley Beal and Damian Lillard, going before Drummond. The center has since proved he deserved to be selected in the top 10. Drummond, now a two-time All-Star, is the biggest threat off the glass in the game. While he may not be the deadliest scorer, his defense makes up for it. Drummond's 6-foot-11, 279-pound body is tough to tackle, and opposing players face an immovable object when playing in the post. He and Blake Griffin now form a two-headed monster up front for the Pistons, and with 2018 Coach of the Year Dwane

Casey now running the show in Motor City, Detroit's poised to make waves in the east.

Drummond has led the league in total rebounds four times, and he ranks first among active players in career rebounds per

game with 13.7. He has also led the league in offensive boards for six straight seasons starting in 2013–14. In the 2017–18 season, while notching a career-best 16 rebounds per game, Drummond became the first

- Named to NBA All-Rookie Second Team in 2012–13
- Has played in two All-Star Games (2016, 2018)
- Named to All-NBA Third Team in 2015–16
- Led the NBA in offensive rebounds for six consecutive seasons (2013–14 to 2018–19)
- Led the NBA in total rebounds for four consecutive seasons (2015–16 to 2018–19)

The Pistons found themselves fighting for the final few playoff spots in the east. Griffin has always been a force — he even scored 50 in 2018–19 — but the man in the middle's consistent play on both ends provided a boost to an up-and-coming Pistons squad desperate to bring a championship to its loyal fans, who have stuck by the team ever since the heyday of Isiah Thomas. The Pistons finished eighth in the east and made the playoffs, squaring off against a dominant Milwaukee Bucks team in the first round. Detroit hadn't won a playoff game in a decade, and the trend continued after the team was swept by the Bucks despite Drummond's posting a double-double in all four games.

Drummond told Forbes in 2019, "I am one of the last true centers," which is probably accurate considering the advent of the point guard and the multitude of three-pointers being hucked up by everyone and their uncle. Even prototypical centers around the league have started chucking threes at will. With only 10 made threes in his career, it's safe to say Drummond is old school. He also plays in an old-school city and even records music in his adopted Motown. The question remains: can he bridge the old and new and bring a championship banner back to Pistons fans?

player since Kevin Garnett in 2004–05 to record 1,000-plus points, 1,000-plus rebounds, 200-plus assists, 100-plus steals and 100-plus blocks. In short, he's been playing his best ball to date, recently adding an offensive arsenal that's seen his season average tick up to over 17 points per game.

In 2018–19 Drummond put up some gaudy numbers, including 26 points and 24 boards early in the season versus the Cleveland Cavs. He followed up that virtuoso performance with 32 points and 17 boards in February versus the Miami Heat, including hitting 8 of 10 from the stripe (Drummond is a career 44.8 percent free-throw shooter, one of the few real knocks on his game). He finished the season with nearly 2 blocks per game, good for top 10 in the league, and once again he led the NBA in rebounding with 15.6 per game.

POSITION POWER FORWARD–SMALL FORWARD / **SHOOTS** RIGHT / **HEIGHT** 6'7" / **WEIGHT** 230 LB. / **DRAFTED** 2012, GOLDEN STATE WARRIORS, 35TH OVERALL

DRAYMOND GREEN 23

DRAYMOND GREEN MUST have been a circus performer in a former life, because he's been walking a tightrope ever since he entered the NBA, shifting between All-Star and agitator. He's emerged as one of the most unique forwards in recent NBA history — blending size, scoring, defensive toughness and a willingness to mix it up with anyone who comes his way. Put simply, there's nobody quite like him.

At 6-foot-7 and 230 pounds, Green's capable of playing both power forward and center, and despite being undersized, he rises to the glass with the ferocity of a bulldog. He's the sparkplug and emotional leader of his team — someone capable of firing himself up and leading his teammates to success. He's already been issued three NBA Finals rings with Golden State. However, this same passion has landed Green in hot water. In 2016 he was dealt an emotional blow when the Warriors blew a 3-1 series lead against Cleveland, and he became Public Enemy Number One to Cavs fans. Some believe it was Green's one-game suspension for kicking LeBron James in Game 4 that sparked the Cavs to victory. His teammates and coaching staff will live with the trash-talking and occasional roughhousing, though — what he brings is the most intangible of intangibles: a motor that doesn't stop firing and a mouth that won't quit. Golden State is fairly confident the shooting prowess of Steph Curry and Klay Thompson can compensate

Finishing his seventh NBA season, Green has put a unique stamp on the league. In 2015–16, he had his strongest season to date, averaging 14 points per game, 9.5 boards and 7.4 assists — flashy numbers for someone who shifts positions so often. He was also a deadly shot from behind the arc, going 39 percent with his 258 three-point attempts. Green put up lofty numbers in 2016–17 as well, leading the league in steals, cracking the top 10 in assists and being named an All-Star. But the craziest stat of the year was the triple-double he posted while scoring only four points (the lowest point total ever for a trip-dub). He was the first since 1986 to record a triple-double that included steals, finishing with 10 assists, 12 rebounds and 10 steals and nearly tying the NBA record of 11 steals in one game.

Even though his offensive numbers dipped after the addition of Kevin Durant, Green still made his presence felt on the court. He finished ninth in assists in the NBA in 2018–19 and averaged just over 7 points and 7 boards a game despite injuries and an early-season argument with Durant that they managed to quash quickly. It may have been a quiet season stat-wise for Green, but the Warriors still finished atop the Western Conference, and in the first round of the postseason versus the crafty LA Clippers, Green posted a triple-double, proving he's still big-time. He only got better as the playoffs went on, recording two straight triple-doubles in the final two games versus Portland. And in Game 4 he and Curry became the first teammates to trip-dub in the same playoff game.

The Warriors have been a modern-day dynasty for years, but the crazy thing is it might not be two-time MVP Steph Curry leading the way. Or the lethal three-point shooter Klay Thompson. It might just be the unsung hero up front, the one who shifts to the middle, slides to the three, sets a pick for his guards and hustles back on defense to steal the rock. It might just be Draymond Green.

CAREER HIGHLIGHTS

- Named NBA Defensive Player of the Year for 2016–17
- Named to NBA All-Defensive First Team three times (2014–15 to 2016–17)
- Has played in three All-Star Games (2016–2018)
- Named to All-NBA Second Team in 2015–16
- Named to All-NBA Third Team in 2016–17

for Green's antics if he gets tossed from another game.

It wasn't an easy road to get to the NBA. In high school, Green was a self-appointed class clown and never studied. He even missed attending an important basketball camp because his mother wouldn't let him go until his grades shot up. They did, and he led his high school team to two state titles in Michigan and earned a scholarship to Michigan State. He stayed all four years there, making it to the Final Four twice, playing in the final in 2009 during his freshman year and winning the Big Ten championship during his senior year. He was drafted 35th overall in 2012 in what now looks like highway robbery. Teams weren't sure how to scout him; he was too short to be a power forward and not fast enough to slide over to small forward. But not being picked until the second round only stoked the burning fire inside one of the NBA's biggest personalities.

NEW ORLEANS PELICANS

POSITION SHOOTING GUARD–POINT GUARD / **SHOOTS** RIGHT / **HEIGHT** 6'4" / **WEIGHT** 205 LB. / **DRAFTED** 2009, PHILADELPHIA 76ERS, 17TH OVERALL

JRUE HOLIDAY  11

SOME PLAYERS ARE destined for greatness the moment they arrive in the NBA. Others take a long, circuitous route to stardom, one season at a time. The latter is true for Jrue Holiday, the New Orleans Pelicans guard who has quietly become one of the best at his position and is turning into a franchise cornerstone in New Orleans.

At 6-foot-4 and 205 pounds, Holiday isn't the biggest or the fastest player. He's more like a hybrid, combining skill, speed and talent into one formidable force.

He does it all. Reliable behind the arc, Holiday has shot over 35 percent since his rookie season in 2009–10. In the 2018–19 season, he averaged 21.2 points per game, the highest of his career. But Holiday's mostly known for his flashy assist totals. He averaged eight a night in his final year in Philly and did the same in the 2018–19 season in NOLA. His role in New Orleans has increased every season, and with the departure of superstar Anthony Davis, who publicly asked for a trade in January 2019 and was traded to the Los Angeles Lakers in the off-season, the Pelicans have quickly become Holiday's team.

In some ways, Holiday was destined to become a baller. Both his parents played in college, and his older brother, Justin, entered the NBA before Jrue followed in his footsteps. His father described Jrue dribbling a basketball with both hands at age 2 — that's seriously impressive. Holiday not only was involved with the basketball team during high school but also moonlighted as the manager of the women's tennis team and as a drummer in the jazz band. Oh, right — *and* he was the 2008 Gatorade National Player of the Year, California's Mr. Basketball and the country's top point guard. Despite the fact that his older brother attended the University of Washington, Holiday chose UCLA to stay close to home. UCLA also has pedigree — NBA stars Kevin Love and Russell Westbrook carved out their

He was traded to New Orleans in 2013, but he sat out half the season because of a stress fracture in his leg. Injuries plagued Holiday during his first three seasons with the Pelicans. He also missed 12 games in 2016–17, but not due to injury. Holiday's wife, a two-time Olympian with the U.S. women's soccer team, was diagnosed with a benign brain tumor that required surgery. She was also pregnant. Putting family first, Holiday took a leave of absence to care for his wife, and luckily everything turned out fine.

Ever since his return, his career has taken off and his stat line has steadily improved. He had a breakout season in 2017–18, averaging 19 points, 6 assists, over 4 rebounds and nearly 50 percent from the field. The team made it to the playoffs under the leadership of Holiday and Davis, going 48-34 and sweeping the Portland Trail Blazers in the first round. The Pels succumbed to the eventual champs, the Golden State Warriors, in five games, but Holiday went out in a blaze, notching a triple-double of 27 points, 10 rebounds and 11 assists in Game 5. It was a disappointing turn of events for Holiday and his Pelicans squad, but for his efforts, he was named to the 2017–18 NBA All-Defensive Team.

The 2018–19 season was his best to date, in which he averaged 21.2 points, 7.7 assists, 5 rebounds and 1.6 steals per game, despite the team's struggles and the in-season distraction of Davis' trade request. He also shot 32.5 percent from behind the arc and 47.2 percent overall from the field. Holiday had his workload reduced in the second half of the season — an abdominal injury sidelined him for the final month — but he's still the Pelicans' focal point going forward. He is signed to a five-year, $131 million contract that runs until 2022. Now a veteran at age 29, Holiday will be tasked with ushering in a new era of young, hungry players. He's expressed that he wants to stay in New Orleans and be a part of the management's decision making going forward. For the Pelicans' management, Holiday might just be the best decision they've ever made.

CAREER HIGHLIGHTS

- Named to NBA All-Defensive First Team in 2017–18
- Named to NBA All-Defensive Second Team in 2018–19
- Played in the 2013 NBA All-Star Game
- Finished in the top 20 in steals five times
- Won the Gatorade National Player of the Year in 2008

careers there, and Holiday continued the trend.

Selected 17th overall by the Philadelphia 76ers in 2009, Holiday started 51 games as a rookie and eventually took over the starting point guard role in his sophomore season, posting 14 points and 6.5 assists per game. He played two more years in Philly and was named an All-Star his final season there.

POSITION SHOOTING GUARD–SMALL FORWARD / **SHOOTS** RIGHT / **HEIGHT** 6'6" / **WEIGHT** 215 LB. / **DRAFTED** 2004, PHILADELPHIA 76ERS, 9TH OVERALL

ANDRE IGUODALA 9

IT'S HARD TO argue the positive impact of a veteran presence on a young team. Sometimes it takes the form of experience on the court, other times, mentorship in the locker room. With Andre Iguodala, his impact shows both on and off the court — a rare combination that helped turn the Golden State Warriors into a powerhouse and the best team in the NBA.

Iguodala was one of the top draft picks in 2004, selected ninth overall by the Philadelphia 76ers. In Philly, he spent eight seasons in a starting role, averaging 40 minutes a night for several seasons in a row while playing alongside legendary point guard Allen Iverson. Iguodala was indispensable on both sides of the court and had his best scoring season in 2007–08, in which he hit the 20-point mark to go along with 5 boards and 5 helpers every game. But Philadelphia was mired in a funk and never escaped the first round of the playoffs until Iguodala's final season with the club. He played one unmemorable season with Denver before landing on the west coast at the beginning of the Splash Brothers era. As long as Iguodala could accept a role off the bench in the latter half of his career, he had the opportunity to flourish again. He did more than just flourish: it was all "Iggy" following his arrival in Oakland.

His numbers have diminished, of course, but his presence as a defensive stopper against the league's best stars has been immeasurable — he made the NBA

- Named NBA Finals MVP in 2015
- Named to NBA All-Rookie First Team in 2004–05
- Named to NBA All-Defensive First Team in 2013–14
- Played in the 2012 NBA All-Star Game
- Won an Olympic gold medal with the U.S. men's basketball team in London in 2012

All-Defensive First Team in 2014 in his early 30s. Undoubtedly, his biggest achievement to date is winning the 2015 NBA championship — his first championship ring and Golden State's first in 40 years. Iguodala was named NBA Finals MVP after guarding LeBron James all series, halting the superstar in his tracks. (Although Iguodala would be on the receiving end the following year, when James ran the length of the court in the final minutes of Game 7 and stuffed Iguodala in what is known as "the Block.")

Raised in Illinois, the small forward played college ball in Arizona, making the Elite Eight his freshman year. After two successful seasons in college, he finished his final year averaging 12.9 points, 8.4 rebounds and 4.9 assists before heading to the big show. Iguodala's strengths are all across the board. He can shoot, defend, post up, play big and play small. His all-around game has made him one of the swingmen on the court. He hits clutch shots, makes clutch stops and always seems to be in the mix. In 2016–17, for example, he dropped 22 points one night versus Memphis, had four steals in a game versus OKC and hauled down 10 boards against Charlotte another night. That's what doing it all means. But most important, he's a calm, veteran voice — always smiling but uber-competitive when it comes to the court. Iguodala was a big part of the team chemistry in Golden State, that chemistry being one of the main reasons Kevin Durant joined the Warriors in 2016–17.

The Warriors won another two championships in 2017 and 2018, and Iguodala slid another couple of rings on his fingers. His numbers the following season, in 2018–19, certainly weren't eye-popping — 5.7 points per game, 3.7 rebounds, 3.2 assists — but that's not how he earns his paycheck. His 23 minutes a night were mostly played on the defensive end, but he chipped in offensively when Durant, Curry or Thompson needed a rest — such as on Christmas Day, when he went 9 of 12 from the field and notched 23 points versus the LA Lakers. With injuries to DeMarcus Cousins and Durant in the 2019 playoffs, Iguodala was forced into a jack-of-all-trades role in the first two rounds, and in the deciding game versus Houston, the 35-year-old played 38 minutes and recorded 17 points and 5 steals in the series win, proving his worth once again.

In the 2019 off-season, the Warriors traded Iguodala to the Memphis Grizzlies, and with his departure it seemed like the end of an era in the Bay area. With many teams vying to land the veteran because of his championship experience and defensive prowess, it's uncertain where Iggy will end up. What is certain is that he has had one of the most consistent NBA careers of the last generation and might just be the most interesting NBA Finals MVP in the history of the league.

KYLE LOWRY [7]

AFTER KYLE LOWRY arrived in Toronto and was thrust into a starting role, the feisty point guard set out to prove everyone wrong. He showed the naysayers that he's got all the talent in the world, he can become the heart and soul of a franchise and he is willing to sacrifice everything for the win.

The Philadelphia native was drafted 24th overall in the 2006 draft by the Memphis Grizzlies after two years at Villanova. But after being passed over by several high-profile teams, the hardscrabble city boy whose father had abandoned him when he was 8 years old stayed close to home and went far away all at once. Alvin Williams, former NBA player and coach at Villanova, described Lowry as "a stubborn, hardnosed kid." But 'Nova needed someone exactly like him: a guard unafraid to drive to the hoop and give them a much-needed edge in the backcourt — things he's still doing in the NBA. Averaging 11 points and 3.7 assists in his sophomore year,

he helped earn a number one seed for Villanova. They lost in the Elite Eight to Florida, and Lowry declared for the NBA.

Built like a Mack truck but blessed with the foot speed of a gazelle, Lowry spent his early years splitting time with other point guards in Memphis and then Houston, skilled players like Mike Conley Jr. and Goran Dragic. He had problems staying healthy, though, due to his hardnosed style of play. After two seasons in Houston, Lowry finally began to flourish, starting 71 games in 2010–11. Not surprisingly he posted then-career bests. But after contracting a bacterial infection, he missed time again and was moved to the Toronto Raptors in the 2012 off-season.

It wasn't a rosy beginning. The Raps still had an established point guard, and Lowry wasn't pleased with being a backup. But a meeting with Raptors now-president Masai Ujiri on the day before training camp transformed Lowry into a different man, and he played like it in 2013–14, lifting the Raptors to the playoffs for the first time in five seasons.

The Raptors gutted it out against the Brooklyn Nets in the 2014 playoffs, taking it to seven games, with Lowry tasked with the game-winning shot. He missed. It stung. But it served notice to the NBA — the Raptors

CAREER HIGHLIGHTS

- Has played in five All-Star Games (2015–2019)
- Named to All-NBA Third Team in 2015–16
- Finished second in assists per game (8.7) in 2018–19
- Finished third in three-point field goals (238) in 2017–18
- Is the Raptors' all-time leader in triple-doubles

multiple triple-doubles and helped lift his squad to first in the Eastern Conference. Unfortunately, he couldn't lift the Raptors past the Cavaliers, who once again swept the Raps in the postseason. Adding salt to the wound, his teammate and best friend, DeMar DeRozan, was traded to San Antonio for Kawhi Leonard. Now it was left up to Lowry to take over the role as the longest serving veteran on a redesigned Raptors squad.

The Raptors won the NBA Finals for the first time in franchise history thanks in part to the leadership of the team's longest-serving player. Against the Milwaukee Bucks in the Eastern Conference finals, Lowry went 7 of 9 from the behind the arc in Game 1, setting the tone for the series and lifting the Raps to its first NBA Finals berth. The court general led the playoffs in charges taken, and his clutch three-point shooting in Game 6 of the NBA Finals (he finished with 26 points and 10 assists) helped send the Warriors packing, earning Lowry the opportunity to hoist the Larry O'Brien trophy as an NBA champion for the first time.

Whether he's chasing down loose balls, knocking down threes or running a play, it appears everyone finally sees the heart and soul that Lowry's always had inside him. His most intangible of intangibles has lifted the Raptors franchise to new heights and pushed them to the highest stratum — NBA champions.

were no joke, and this was Lowry's team, live or die. He has owned the role of emotional heartbeat for the franchise ever since.

Among point guards, Lowry hangs out with the leaders in assist-to-turnover ratio and consistently changes the outcomes of games with his defensive tenacity and timely steals. In 2015–16 he led the Raps deep into the playoffs to the Eastern Conference finals. In 2016–17, Lowry continued soaring upward — his average point total increased to 22.4 and his three-point

shooting surpassed 40 percent as the Raps made the playoffs for the fourth straight year. He ended his run at the championship with a sprained ankle and watched from the sidelines as the Cleveland Cavaliers swept the Raptors in the second round.

The once-disgruntled point guard finally learned to trust his coaches, his teammates and ultimately himself, signing a three-year, $100 million contract with the Raptors in the 2017 off-season. To punctuate the deal, Lowry dropped a 40-point game and

POSITION SHOOTING GUARD / SHOOTS RIGHT / HEIGHT 6'3" / WEIGHT 190 LB. / DRAFTED 2013, PORTLAND TRAIL BLAZERS, 10TH OVERALL

C.J. McCOLLUM

C.J. MCCOLLUM HAS finally arrived. The 6-foot-3 shooting guard was named the 2015–16 Most Improved Player, but he hasn't stopped there. The Portland shooting guard is one of the up-and-coming stars in the NBA. If 2015–16 was his breakout hit

single, McCollum's new claim to fame is that he has stayed at the top of the charts ever since.

It's always been an uphill battle for the once-diminutive Portland Trail Blazers shooting guard. It wasn't lack of talent

but lack of size that held him back — McCollum stood just 5-foot-2 in his freshman year of high school. A late bloomer, he shot up in stature and played a starring role for Glen Oak High School in Canton, Ohio, once recording 54 points in a single game. "When you're smaller, you kind of learn how to do other things," McCollum said in 2013. "You have to work a little bit harder. Nothing really comes easy to you when you're under-recruited . . . undersized . . . undervalued. You have to be better than the bigger guys." McCollum was always in the gym, committed to getting bigger and stronger. His desire to win no matter what the cost was quickly evident; he even broke down crying one night on the floor during his first year of college, blaming himself for letting the older players down — something his coaches took as a sign of maturity. They knew they had a special player on their hands.

His passion paid off and McCollum proved his worth immediately, taking the relatively unknown Lehigh Mountain Hawks all the way to the 2010 NCAA tournament, where he stroked 26 points as a freshman in his first contest on the national stage. McCollum returned to the tournament two years later, knocking off second-seeded powerhouse Duke while leading the 15th-seeded Lehigh to a huge upset win. He stayed all four years at college, completing his journalism degree before being drafted 10th overall in the 2013 NBA Draft.

Although McCollum didn't see regular minutes for several seasons in Portland, the talent and the sweet stroke were there, and he went off for nearly 40 percent from behind the arc in his first two seasons.

His meteoric rise in the NBA coincided with receiving regular playing time, which shouldn't come as a surprise. But going from 6.8 points per game in his second season off the bench to over 20 a night as a starter in his third season — one of the largest increases for one player between seasons — caused quite a stir and led to his Most Improved Player award. In 11 games during the 2015–16 playoffs, he played more than 40 minutes a game, averaging over 20 points a night. He also provided fellow guard

Damian Lillard with the backcourt help he'd long needed.

McCollum bettered his breakout campaign in 2016–17. In the first half of the season, he scalded the Pacers with 34 points, including seven threes. On New Year's Day, he dropped 43 points versus Minnesota. McCollum's three-point shooting is getting even better, and his free-throw shooting was flirting with 90 percent all 2016–17.

The 2017–18 and 2018–19 seasons were no different. With Lillard as the driver, McCollum's been patiently sitting shotgun, chipping in around 21 points a game in both seasons and hitting over 37 percent of his three-point attempts. Portland went 53-29 in 2018–19 (good for third in the west), and McCollum twice put up 40-point games. Portland slayed Russell Westbrook and the Oklahoma City Thunder in the first round of the postseason, and it seemed like the Trail Blazers had finally turned a corner.

The proof in the pudding was reaching round three of the playoffs after a back-and-forth seven-game series against the Denver Nuggets, with McCollum proving to the league that he and Lillard are a force to be reckoned with.

It's not all rosy though. McCollum needs to work on getting his assists and rebounds totals up — under five per game won't cut it in superstar land — but because his lights-out shooting keeps contributing to wins and playoff appearances, there's plenty of time to develop a full arsenal in the coming years.

Portland is still short of topping the tough Western Conference, but when LaMarcus Aldridge departed in 2015, the torch was passed to the backcourt. Rip City has a new lieutenant in C.J. McCollum, and it's time to salute one of the NBA's rising stars. No. 3 looks as if he belongs with the top shooters in the game, and he's also under contract until 2021 — something Trail Blazers fans should be thrilled about.

POSITION POINT GUARD / **SHOOTS** RIGHT / **HEIGHT** 6'1" / **WEIGHT** 184 LB. / **DRAFTED** 2011, CHARLOTTE HORNETS, 9TH OVERALL

KEMBA WALKER  8

KEMBA HUDLEY WALKER of the Bronx, New York, burst onto the scene suddenly, like a house on fire — a small but tough point guard who could score at will no matter what the level. Since he landed in the league, Walker has pulled the Charlotte Hornets franchise like a lead pack dog but now faces a new challenge as the star point guard for the Boston Celtics. Success or failure will fall on the shoulders of Walker, who has proven size doesn't matter when you're all heart.

Walker made a name for himself on the national stage playing in the NCAA Final Four, carrying the UConn Huskies to the championship in 2011 during his junior year. Walker was on fire, dropping 150 points en route to the Big East title, and he continued his hot streak while leading the third-seeded Huskies past Butler in the NCAA final. During the 2011 Big East tourney, UConn put up five wins in five days. What followed was an undefeated run to cast Walker into NCAA lore. It's arguably one of the hottest runs a college player's ever put together, and Walker was named outstanding player of the tournament. He elected to enter the NBA Draft and was selected ninth overall by the Michael Jordan–owned Charlotte Hornets (then known as the Bobcats).

What makes Walker so damn good? You could say it's all in the footwork. As a youth he possessed not only blinding speed on the court but also coordination

that led him to moonlight as a dancer at the famed Apollo Theater. (Hence the crazy amount of space he creates on his patented step-back.) Growing up in the hard-nosed Bronx is tough enough, but to be the best and rise above you have to play your guts

out. And every time, there was Walker, like lightning to the basket. Legend has it he scored 80 points one game without hitting a single three.

In his first three seasons as a full-time starter in Charlotte, Walker was remarkably

consistent, averaging just over 17 points a game. But Charlotte was doing poorly and finished the lockout-shortened 2011–12 season 7-59, the worst winning percentage in NBA history. The freshly drafted Walker took the losses hard after his college successes the year before. "It [was] killing me," he recalled in 2016 when asked about his rookie season.

Walker went to work, fixing his jump shot and three-point angles instead of polishing a predictable dribble-and-drive game. His shooting percentage increased, and things in Charlotte started to improve under a new head coach. The basket-first point guard is atypical in that he's not an assist-first guy, but he has learned to share the ball with his teammates while still driving to the basket like he did in the Bronx. In the past four seasons he's elevated his game to become one of the NBA's must-watch stars, and he now averages nearly 26 points a night. The difference? Bust-out games, like the 40-10-7 stat line he ripped against Toronto early in the 2016–17 season, or the 38 points he dropped and the 6 assists he dished in January 2018 against Atlanta.

Walker played in his first All-Star Game in 2017, and that's always a time for reflection, especially for an underappreciated, undersized guard whom people had always doubted. He's now played in the All-Star Game three times, finally earning the recognition that a player of his caliber deserves.

In 2018–19, Walker finished top 10 in scoring (25.6) and top 20 in assists (5.9). He also entered the 60 club when he put up a ridiculous 60 points on 21-of-34 shooting in an OT loss versus Philadelphia in November. Charlotte made another late charge for the playoffs, but the team fell just short despite Walker's 43 in the last game of the season and his 47 on the board just weeks prior. He was named Eastern Conference Player of the Week to end the season.

With his Hornets contract ending in 2019, Walker departed the only franchise he's ever known for the storied Boston

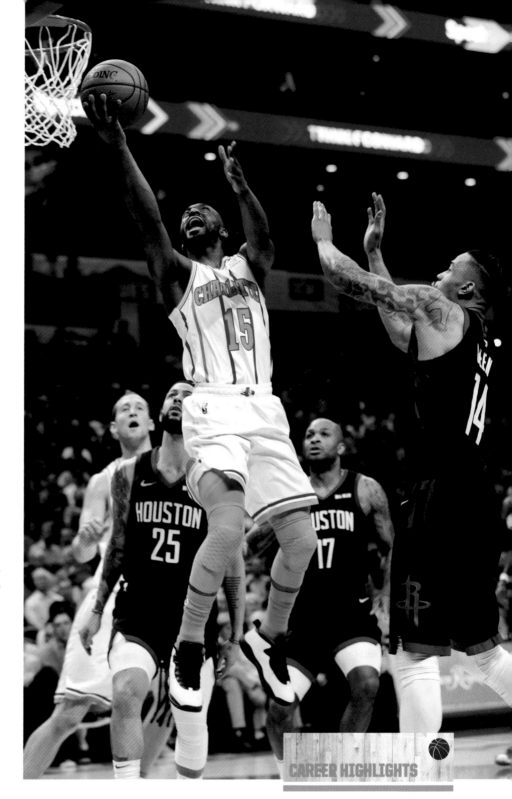

CAREER HIGHLIGHTS

Celtics. He signed up for four years, $141 million and a chance at a fresh start with a team used to being at the top.

Perhaps the coolest thing about Walker is how multitalented he is — singing, rapping and dancing off the court, he's an infectious personality with a big smile. The footwork's always been there, as has the bounce in his step, and just like he did when he was playing on the tough courts of New York, he continues to defy the odds.

- Has played in three All-Star Games (2017–2019)
- Named to All-NBA Third Team in 2018–19
- Finished third in field goals (731) and points (2,101) in 2018–19
- Is a seven-time NBA Player of the Week
- Named Final Four Most Outstanding Player in 2011

NBA REGULAR-SEASON MVP WINNERS

2018–19: Giannis Antetokounmpo, Milwaukee Bucks

2017–18: James Harden, Houston Rockets

2016–17: Russell Westbrook, Oklahoma City Thunder

2015–16: Stephen Curry, Golden State Warriors

2014-15: Stephen Curry, Golden State Warriors

2013-14: Kevin Durant, Oklahoma City Thunder

2012-13: LeBron James, Miami Heat

2011-12: LeBron James, Miami Heat

2010-11: Derrick Rose, Chicago Bulls

2009-10: LeBron James, Cleveland Cavaliers

2008-09: LeBron James, Cleveland Cavaliers

2007-08: Kobe Bryant, Los Angeles Lakers

2006-07: Dirk Nowitzki, Dallas Mavericks

2005-06: Steve Nash, Phoenix Suns

2004-05: Steve Nash, Phoenix Suns

2003-04: Kevin Garnett, Minnesota Timberwolves

2002-03: Tim Duncan, San Antonio Spurs

2001-02: Tim Duncan, San Antonio Spurs

2000-01: Allen Iverson, Philadelphia 76ers

1999-00: Shaquille O'Neal, Los Angeles Lakers

1998-99: Karl Malone, Utah Jazz

1997-98: Michael Jordan, Chicago Bulls

1996-97: Karl Malone, Utah Jazz

1995-96: Michael Jordan, Chicago Bulls

1994-95: David Robinson, San Antonio Spurs

1993-94: Hakeem Olajuwon, Houston Rockets

1992-93: Charles Barkley, Phoenix Suns

1991-92: Michael Jordan, Chicago Bulls

1990-91: Michael Jordan, Chicago Bulls

1989-90: Earvin Johnson, Los Angeles Lakers

1988-89: Earvin Johnson, Los Angeles Lakers

1987-88: Michael Jordan, Chicago Bulls

1986-87: Earvin Johnson, Los Angeles Lakers

1985-86: Larry Bird, Boston Celtics

1984-85: Larry Bird, Boston Celtics

1983-84: Larry Bird, Boston Celtics

1982-83: Moses Malone, Philadelphia 76ers

1981-82: Moses Malone, Houston Rockets

1980-81: Julius Erving, Philadelphia 76ers

1979-80: Kareem Abdul-Jabbar, Los Angeles Lakers

1978-79: Moses Malone, Houston Rockets

1977-78: Bill Walton, Portland Trail Blazers

1976-77: Kareem Abdul-Jabbar, Los Angeles Lakers

1975-76: Kareem Abdul-Jabbar, Los Angeles Lakers

1974-75: Bob McAdoo, Buffalo Braves

1973-74: Kareem Abdul-Jabbar, Milwaukee Bucks

1972-73: Dave Cowens, Boston Celtics

1971-72: Kareem Abdul-Jabbar, Milwaukee Bucks

1970-71: Kareem Abdul-Jabbar, Milwaukee Bucks

1969-70: Willis Reed, New York Knicks

1968-69: Wes Unseld, Baltimore Bullets

1967-68: Wilt Chamberlain, Philadelphia 76ers

1966-67: Wilt Chamberlain, Philadelphia 76ers

1965-66: Wilt Chamberlain, Philadelphia 76ers

1964-65: Bill Russell, Boston Celtics

1963-64: Oscar Robertson, Cincinnati Royals

1962-63: Bill Russell, Boston Celtics

1961-62: Bill Russell, Boston Celtics

1960-61: Bill Russell, Boston Celtics

1959-60: Wilt Chamberlain, Philadelphia Warriors

1958-59: Bob Pettit,
St. Louis Hawks

1957-58: Bill Russell,
Boston Celtics

1956-57: Bob Cousy,
Boston Celtics

1955-56: Bob Pettit,
St. Louis Hawks

Six-time regular-season MVP
Kareem Abdul-Jabbar of the
Los Angeles Lakers scores
two points in the 1980 Western
Conference semifinals against
the Phoenix Suns.

NBA ALL-STAR GAME MVP WINNERS

2018–19: Kevin Durant, Golden State Warriors

2017–18: LeBron James, Cleveland Cavaliers

2016–17: Anthony Davis, New Orleans Pelicans

2015–16: Russell Westbrook, Oklahoma City Thunder

2014–15: Russell Westbrook, Oklahoma City Thunder

2013–14: Kyrie Irving, Cleveland Cavaliers

2012-13: Chris Paul, Los Angeles Clippers

2011-12: Kevin Durant, Oklahoma City Thunder

2010-11: Kobe Bryant, Los Angeles Lakers

2009-10: Dwyane Wade, Miami Heat

2008-09: Shaquille O'Neal, Phoenix Suns (Tie)

2008-09: Kobe Bryant, Los Angeles Lakers (Tie)

2007-08: LeBron James, Cleveland Cavaliers

2006-07: Kobe Bryant, Los Angeles Lakers

2005-06: LeBron James, Cleveland Cavaliers

2004-05: Allen Iverson, Philadelphia 76ers

2003-04: Shaquille O'Neal, Los Angeles Lakers

2002-03: Kevin Garnett, Minnesota Timberwolves

2001-02: Kobe Bryant, Los Angeles Lakers

2000-01: Allen Iverson, Philadelphia 76ers

1999-00: Shaquille O'Neal, Los Angeles Lakers (Tie)

1999-00: Tim Duncan, San Antonio Spurs (Tie)

1997-98: Michael Jordan, Chicago Bulls

1996-97: Glen Rice, Charlotte Hornets

1995-96: Michael Jordan, Chicago Bulls

1994-95: Mitch Richmond, Sacramento Kings

1993-94: Scottie Pippen, Chicago Bulls

1992-93: John Stockton, Utah Jazz (Tie)

1992-93: Karl Malone, Utah Jazz (Tie)

1991-92: Earvin Johnson, Los Angeles Lakers

1990-91: Charles Barkley, Philadelphia 76ers

1989-90: Earvin Johnson, Los Angeles Lakers

1988-89: Karl Malone, Utah Jazz

1987-88: Michael Jordan, Chicago Bulls

1986-87: Tom Chambers, Seattle SuperSonics

1985-86: Isiah Thomas, Detroit Pistons

1984-85: Ralph Sampson, Houston Rockets

1983-84: Isiah Thomas, Detroit Pistons

1982-83: Julius Erving, Philadelphia 76ers

1981-82: Larry Bird, Boston Celtics

1980-81: Nate Archibald, Boston Celtics

1979-80: George Gervin, San Antonio Spurs

1978-79: David Thompson, Denver Nuggets

1977-78: Randy Smith, Buffalo Braves

1976-77: Julius Erving, Philadelphia 76ers

1975-76: Dave Bing, Washington Bullets

1974-75: Walt Frazier, New York Knicks

1973-74: Bob Lanier, Detroit Pistons

1972-73: Dave Cowens, Boston Celtics

1971-72: Jerry West, Los Angeles Lakers

1970-71: Lenny Wilkens, Seattle SuperSonics

1969-70: Willis Reed, New York Knicks

1968-69: Oscar Robertson, Cincinnati Royals

1967-68: Hal Greer, Philadelphia 76ers

1966-67: Rick Barry, San Francisco Warriors

1965-66: Adrian Smith, Cincinnati Royals

1964-65: Jerry Lucas, Cincinnati Royals

1963-64: Oscar Robertson, Cincinnati Royals

1962-63: Bill Russell, Boston Celtics

1961-62: Bob Pettit, St. Louis Hawks

1960-61: Oscar Robertson,
Cincinnati Royals

1959-60: Wilt Chamberlain,
Philadelphia Warriors

1958-59: Bob Pettit,
St. Louis Hawks (Tie)

1958-59: Elgin Baylor,
Minneapolis Lakers (Tie)

1957-58: Bob Pettit,
St. Louis Hawks

1956-57: Bob Cousy,
Boston Celtics

1955-56: Bob Pettit,
St. Louis Hawks

1954-55: Bill Sharman,
Boston Celtics

1953-54: Bob Cousy,
Boston Celtics

1952-53: George Mikan,
Minneapolis Lakers

1951-52: Paul Arizin,
Philadelphia Warriors

1950-51: Ed Macauley,
Boston Celtics

Three-time All-Star Game
MVP Michael Jordan of the
Chicago Bulls slam dunks
the ball.

NBA FINALS MVP WINNERS

2018–19: Kawhi Leonard, Toronto Raptors

2017–18: Kevin Durant, Golden State Warriors

2016–17: Kevin Durant, Golden State Warriors

2015–16: LeBron James, Cleveland Cavaliers

2014-15: Andre Iguodala, Golden State Warriors

2013-14: Kawhi Leonard, San Antonio Spurs

2012-13: LeBron James, Miami Heat

2011-12: LeBron James, Miami Heat

2010-11: Dirk Nowitzki, Dallas Mavericks

2009-10: Kobe Bryant, Los Angeles Lakers

2008-09: Kobe Bryant, Los Angeles Lakers

2007-08: Paul Pierce, Boston Celtics

2006-07: Tony Parker, San Antonio Spurs

2005-06: Dwyane Wade, Miami Heat

2004-05: Tim Duncan, San Antonio Spurs

2003-04: Chauncey Billups, Detroit Pistons

2002-03: Tim Duncan, San Antonio Spurs

2001-02: Shaquille O'Neal, Los Angeles Lakers

2000-01: Shaquille O'Neal, Los Angeles Lakers

1999-00: Shaquille O'Neal, Los Angeles Lakers

1998-99: Tim Duncan, San Antonio Spurs

1997-98: Michael Jordan, Chicago Bulls

1996-97: Michael Jordan, Chicago Bulls

1995-96: Michael Jordan, Chicago Bulls

1994-95: Hakeem Olajuwon, Houston Rockets

1993-94: Hakeem Olajuwon, Houston Rockets

1992-93: Michael Jordan, Chicago Bulls

1991-92: Michael Jordan, Chicago Bulls

1990-91: Michael Jordan, Chicago Bulls

1989-90: Isiah Thomas, Detroit Pistons

1988-89: Joe Dumars, Detriot Pistons

1987-88: James Worthy, Los Angeles Lakers

1986-87: Earvin Johnson, Los Angeles Lakers

1985-86: Larry Bird, Boston Celtics

1984-85: Kareem Abdul-Jabbar, Los Angeles Lakers

1983-84: Larry Bird, Boston Celtics

1982-83: Moses Malone, Philadelphia 76ers

1981-82: Earvin Johnson, Los Angeles Lakers

1980-81: Cedric Maxwell, Boston Celtics

1979-80: Earvin Johnson, Los Angeles Lakers

1978-79: Dennis Johnson, Seattle SuperSonics

1977-78: Wes Unseld, Washington Bullets

1976-77: Bill Walton, Portland Trail Blazers

1975-76: Jo Jo White, Boston Celtics

1974-75: Rick Barry, Golden State Warriors

1973-74: John Havlicek, Boston Celtics

1972-73: Willis Reed, New York Knicks

1971-72: Wilt Chamberlain, Los Angeles Lakers

1970-71: Kareem Abdul-Jabbar, Milwaukee Bucks

1969-70: Willis Reed, New York Knicks

1968-69: Jerry West, Los Angeles Lakers

Two-time finals MVP Kevin Durant of the Golden State Warriors dunks over LeBron James of the Cleveland Cavaliers in Game 3 of the 2017 NBA Finals.

ACKNOWLEDGMENTS

FIRST, I'D LIKE to thank my editors, Steve Cameron and Julie Takasaki, whose sharp eyes for detail and ability to come up with multiple ways of saying rebounds and assists are exceptional qualities. Their patience, guidance and steady hands are all over this book. I'd like to express my gratitude to publisher Lionel Koffler and all the staff at Firefly Books, as well as copyeditor Patricia MacDonald and designer Matt Filion, for their help in molding and shaping *Basketball Now!* — books are very much a collaboration, and the hard work of everyone involved is much appreciated.

Personally, I'd like to thank my parents, David and Esther-Jo, and my sister, Michelle, whose support has always been unwavering. While many friends and former colleagues have inspired me while writing this book, I'd like to particularly thank everyone who has watched basketball with me over the past several seasons, especially during the Raptors' epic run to the franchise's first NBA championship in its 24-year history. I'd like to give a special shout-out to two of my oldest friends, Josh and Micah, for all those games of horse and twenty-one in my alleyway when we were kids growing up in Vancouver (RIP Grizzlies). For many kids like me, those moments formed the nucleus of my earliest basketball memories (beyond the Bulls' first three-peat and the Grizzlies' franchise-changing drafting of Bryant "Big Country" Reeves). I can think of nothing better than spending a lazy summer afternoon shooting hoops in the sun, and it was during those formative years that I learned what it means to love sport, friends and lazy days on the courts. Finally, I'd like to thank you, the basketball fan, for reading!

– Adam Elliott Segal

Kawhi Leonard of the Toronto Raptors blocks Stephen Curry of the Golden State Warriors in Game 3 of the 2019 NBA Finals, the Raptors' first run at the championship title in franchise history.

PROFILE INDEX

PHOTO CREDITS

AP PHOTO

AP Photo: 34, 153
Aaron Gash: 13
Ben Margot: 6–7, 45
Bill Kostroun: 95
Brandon Dill: 29, 109, 136
Butch Dill: 142
Carlos Osorio: 76, 138
Charles Krupa: 118, 119
Chris Szagola: 48, 117
Chuck Burton: 83, 135, 151
Craig Mitchelldyer: 72, 148, 149
Danny Karnik: 105
Darren Abate: 28, 42
Darron Cummings: 51
David Dermer: 57
David J. Phillip: 9, 79
Diane Bondareff: 37
Duane Burleson: 52, 53
Elise Amendola: 12, 38–39
Eric Christian Smith: 15, 20, 140
Eric Risberg: 131
Frank Franklin II: 77, 147
George Widman: 36
Gerald Herbert: 97
Greg Wahl-Stephens: 92–93, 94
Harold P. Matosian: 129
Joel Auerbach: 70–71
John Amis: 22, 121
John Raoux: 26, 82, 89
Kevin Hagen: 27
Mark J. Terrill: 24, 87
Marty Lederhandler: 32–33
Mary Altaffer: 4–5
Matt Slocum: 81
Michael Conroy: 23, 43
Michael Dwyer: 10–11
Michael Wyke: 84
Mike Roemer: 115
Mike Stone: 128
Nam Y. Huh: 108
Nick Wass: 44, 61, 103, 134
Paul Sancya: 139
Peter Southwick: 96
Rich Pedroncelli: 40–41, 107
Rick Bowmer: 78, 100–101, 111
Rick Scuteri: 74, 86
Rob Ferguson: 88
Scott Troyanos: 126
Steve Yeater: 120
Sue Ogrocki: 31, 54, 132–133

Susan Sterner: 35
Tim Johnson: 130
Tony Dejak: 58, 157
Wilfredo Lee: 75
Willie J. Allen Jr.: 91

GETTY IMAGES

Bettmann / Contributor: 127
Bill Smith / NBAE: 67
Carl Iwasaki / Sports Ilustrated: 65
Jesse D. Garrabant / NBAE: 68–69
Nathaniel S. Butler / NBAE: 62–63, 64
Walter Iooss Jr. / Sports Illustrated: 66

ICON SPORTSWIRE

Brian Rothmuller: 14, 16, 18, 19, 21, 25, 30, 46, 47, 50, 55, 59, 60, 73, 80, 90, 102, 106, 112, 114, 123, 141, 143, 144, 150
Daniel Kucin Jr.: 56
Hector Acevedo / Zuma Press: 85, 104, 113, 116
Icon Sportswire: 99, 122, 146
Kevin Reece: 155
Kevin Sullivan / Zuma Press: 98
Kyle Ross: 49
PI / Zuma Press: 110
Prensa Internacional / Zuma Press: 124–125, 137, 158
Ray Chavez / Zuma Press: 2
Stephen Lew: 17, 145

Front Cover:

Adam Davis/Icon Sportswire (Antetokounmpo)
Brian Rothmuller/Icon Sportswire (James, Durant, Curry, Harden)
Ezra Shaw, Pool/AP Photo (Leonard)

Back Cover:

Brian Rothmuller/Icon Sportswire (Doncic, Lillard)
Hector Acevedo/Zuma Press/Icon Sportswire (Murray)

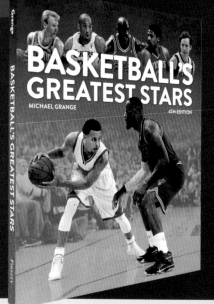
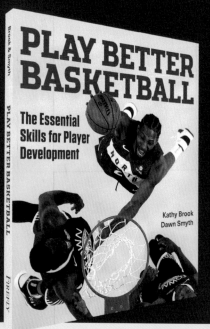